COSTLY ROOTS

SARAH COHEN

CROSSBRIDGE BOOKS

Dedication

Dedicated to my son Matthew,
with infinite love and thanks
for being exactly how you are.

I especially praise God for my husband Eric,
for without his input, patience and tremendous
encouragement I would never have been able
to complete this book.

Acknowledgements

I am grateful to the Rev. David Collinson for his foreword.

I wish to thank Mrs Sandra Levy for her patience in coping with my longhand manuscript and for typing it.

Praise and thanksgiving, above all, to God Himself, Father, Son and Holy Spirit, who makes all things possible in His Love. This book is about Him and how He has worked. I pray He will bless all who read it.

To protect those mentioned in the book I have changed the names and places where embarrassment could be caused; otherwise, it is as completely factual as my memory will allow.

Sarah Cohen.

FOREWORD

Back in the early 1970s, when I was a Methodist Minister in a little Yorkshire mill town, a newly married couple began to attend my church. They were not exactly young, though the wife, a vivacious, dark-eyed woman, seemed much younger than her husband. Both were smart, likeable, intelligent and deeply committed to the Lord Jesus Christ. At the same time I sensed that both had already led full lives before God brought them together. Just how full a life Sarah Cohen, the wife, had led becomes apparent in these pages. Later, they joined a fellowship group, which my wife and I ran at the manse, and it was after one of those meetings that we prayed for the baby boy Sarah was carrying, with results I'll leave you to discover as you read the story!

It was not long before we moved away, and our paths have not often crossed since then, but Sarah has kept in touch with us, and it has been a delight to discover how she has been carving out a ministry for herself as a Christian writer — and it is a ministry. The book you now have in your hand is a collection of scenes from her life story, a wide-ranging pilgrimage as God led this feisty, somewhat rebellious girl out of her Jewish home, then through a wilderness period, followed by her meeting with her husband, a growing tranquillity, before spending time in the USA.

Sometimes the story she tells is hilarious, sometimes upsetting, but it is always interesting, and one thing is certain: when you pick up the book, give yourself plenty of time, because you really won't be able to put it down!

Rev. David Collinson,
Retired Superintendent Methodist Minister.

Contents

1

Buried Alive?

For the tears that flow in secret
In the broken times;
For the moments of elation
Or the troubled mind —

(Graham Kendrick)

Footsteps reverberated along the length of the corridor, coming to a stop outside the confines of my room in the Nurses' Home. Opening the door, I saw the space was almost filled by the bulk of a staff nurse, clad in the regulation light blue uniform. Meeting her large chocolate brown eyes, my mouth eased instinctively into a small smile, trying not to betray my true feelings of apprehension.

'Sarah, I only received your note today —'

'Please,' I said steadily. 'Please, Lois, do come in.'

'You have something on your mind?'

'Yeah. Well, yes I have.'

Lois rolled her eyes under long jet-black lashes. 'Look, it's quite late and I've had one awful day ... so get on with it.'

I pulled a wry face. 'Oh, oh I'm sorry,' I said, breaking in

sympathetically. 'It's just I've been trying to reach you for a couple of days. And what I've got to say is strictly for your ears only. Okay?'

My friend heaved a deep breath and hoisted her somewhat overweight body heavily down onto my single divan, a slight trace of displeasure in her attractive dark features. 'I've been busy. Anyway, if you've got some sort of a problem could you just spit it out, eh?'

I nodded. 'It's really more of a favour than a problem ...'

'Okay, but I'd really like coffee first,' she said. 'Black with no sugar. I'm on a diet!'

Since the beginning of our nurse training, three and a half years previously, Lois Thomas, who'd become one of my closest friends, was always on some sort of a failed diet. Although most of her family were still over in Kingston, Jamaica, she had an Uncle Julius living in Haydons Road in Wimbledon; Julius had opened up his home to her, treating her like a daughter.

'I was wondering ... when will you next be visiting him?'

Lois shrugged. 'Probably next week. I'm not sure. Why do you want to know?'

My voice wobbled a little. 'It's about a headstone.'

'A headstone! Whose headstone are we talking about?'

'Mine, I think.'

'Yours!' Lois snorted, casting a gaze of sudden irritation. 'Aw, look, if this is some kind of wind-up ... I'm not in the mood for silly jokes.'

I slumped in my armchair with a weary sigh and began to relate my story — something I'd managed previously to keep quiet.

I told her how the crunch came about six months after my conversion to Christianity.

In February of 1963, three months before I was seventeen, I'd read in Acts 8:36-39 about the Ethiopian eunuch's baptism. I decided I would also be baptised — to be fully

immersed in water.

I was already a little out of favour with my family, for my conversion to Christianity had become almost a major source of discord in the family. My Auntie Maggie, Dad's sister, tried to talk me out of being a Christian without any success. In vain, I explained about my new-found faith both to her and my parents, including my maternal grandfather, yet they didn't even want to understand.

'But,' I sighed, 'by accepting Jesus I can have eternal life.'

They took no notice; neither would I of them. I had dug my heels in.

I waited for what I thought was the right moment, when Mum and Dad were sitting together in the living room. Hesitantly, I sat beside Dad. I informed them both of my plans to be baptised.

Mum put aside her sewing basket. 'If you go ahead with this stupid ritual, then you cannot be one of us any more. Do you hear me?' she sniped in hard denunciation. It was quite clear to her that what I intended to do was similar to a Jew being mikvahed — a form of total immersion in water, usually in a part of the synagogue, declaring one's Jewish beliefs by a ritual cleansing.

I shook my head. 'That's just plain nasty. Couldn't you even *try* to see it from my point of view?' I replied. 'For me it's so important to be baptised. It's a sort of witness to what I now believe.'

'Has this all stemmed from your time in St Anthony's Hospital?' Dad asked, remembering when I had my appendix removed. 'Is it to do with the nun? You're not going to be a ... a Catholic through what's her name ...?'

I shook my head. 'You mean Sister Helen Curmi? However, I did find out who Jesus was ... Helen told me about Him.'

It all started at the hospital's visiting time on a Monday

3

afternoon. Mum was making her way along the corridor to the women's surgical ward. Pulling up a wooden chair close to my bedside, she glanced sideways, dragging her mind in the direction of the next bed, earning herself a broad smile from the nun occupying it.

'She's really nice,' I remarked. 'I really like her a lot.'

Quickly snuffing out any admiration, Mum gave an unladylike snort and averted her dark eyes. 'The woman's a nun, for heaven's sake! You've absolutely nothing in common with any of them ... not with Catholics ... oh, Sarah, be sensible.'

The arrogance and ungodly spirit of my mother caused me to put her words down to a sort of disgust. As my aggravating appendix was like a prolonged hailstorm battering the lower right side of my abdomen, I felt too unwell to engage upon a 'situation' with her.

The next morning my nun was checked over by an anaesthetist and, breakfast refused, she was whisked off to the operating theatre, also for an appendectomy.

Days passed and she and I could look upon one another with abdomen-clutching empathy. However, at the commencement of each following day, before her breakfast, she would be screened off from me. This caused me to peek with curiosity through the cracks in the screen.

'She keeps having some sort of a one-way conversation with someone named Jesus Christ,' I told my father when he came to visit me. 'What do you think she's up to with him then?'

He shrugged. 'How on earth should I know, eh?'

The ten post-operative days meant time off High School. I was sixteen and eventually planning on enrolling as a foundation student at Wimbledon College of Art and Design.

'May I sketch you, Sister? Just your head and shoulders ... okay?'

She nodded, a broad grin across her face.

4

'Keep still then, please. Oh, and by the way, may I ask who Jesus is? You keep talking to him, don't you? Is he from Malta ... a bit like you?'

Her chocolate brown eyes were smiling, she making a great effort not to laugh. Then her velvet tones held a more serious note, yet almost with an excitement as she told me something about her Christianity ... of Christ and her God.

Before she was able to explain any more, however, someone coming from the opposite direction caught my eye. An older man, maybe about fifty, was smiling at me.

'Hallo.' He came up and stood beside me. 'How are you?'

I shrugged. 'I'm here because of my appendix.'

The man had clear, blue eyes, and something about the way he looked at me made me feel as though I'd known him forever in a comfortable way.

'I'm the Rev. John Clifford ... one of the hospital chaplains.' He hesitated a minute, and a smile played on his lips as he leaned over my sketch of the nun.

'It's very good!' he exclaimed, and then explained that he was a Methodist minister at a fairly large church in Wimbledon, just a stone's throw from where I lived with my parents.

'Come and see us once you're better, m'dear.'

'I don't know if I shall. You see, I don't know anything about church and all that stuff.'

He visited me again, just before my discharge home. During the second visit he informed me a little more about Jesus and also concerning the origins of Methodism.

Before he left he tightened the grip he had on my hand. 'Close your eyes, and I'll pray,' he said. And, in a fatherly sort of way, having prayed, he gave me a peck on the side of my face.

About a year later I approached the late Dr D. Martyn Lloyd-Jones. He was the eminent minister of London's

Westminster Chapel.

'Ah, now,' he began. 'I do sometimes baptise adults, but it's only by sprinkling water on them. I don't immerse them in a pool.'

'I wish to be fully immersed just like the Ethiopian eunuch,' I replied.

The minister shook his head. 'You might be better finding a Baptist church nearer to where you live.'

I did, yet it was at a difficult family time.

My father, by then, was also recovering from surgery. His gall bladder had been removed, along with one lobe of his left lung. Because he was then an undiagnosed haemophiliac, throughout the operation he had bled heavily, leaving him with an incisional intestinal hernia, a large lump over the scar. Following his enforced convalescent period, he mostly lay on the sofa in the dining room; too bone tired to be bothered to dress, remaining in his warm dressing gown. He appeared unusually thin and pale, content to be fed with only either warm drinks or strained soup.

'I'm thinking about being baptised,' I started, telling my mother.

'It's a bad time. What with Dad being so poorly and ... be sensible ...' her dark eyes glaring at me like a raging storm. 'And surely you can wait, can't you?'

I shrugged. 'What difference would it make to either you or Dad, huh? What I do on a Sunday seems to be entirely up to me.'

'I need you here.'

'What for?'

'To help, of course. I can't do everything for Dad by myself. Why else?'

My father felt the heat flooding to his face and his jaws clamped together before raising his head a little by one of the cotton-covered cushions. His weakened voice apologised for causing so much trouble before his eyelids dropped, allowing

him to soon nod off into a bit of a snooze.

While he slept Mum and I crept out into the small breakfast room and sat either side of the fire. She reached down, poked it and shovelled on some of the dusty coal. I gave it another obliging poke.

'Why have you got so involved with the Baptist Church? We never intended you —'

Before I could reply she reminded me of how I'd been confirmed at All Saints Anglican Church in South Wimbledon.

'I was only thirteen. I didn't understand what it was all about. I had no idea and I did it only to accompany a friend,' I explained. 'You remember Sue ...'

'Yeah. Well at least you only went once. And then there was South Wimbledon Methodist Church. Why there?'

'The minister listened to me. He was okay.'

'And I suppose we don't?'

I leaned backward and said, 'And the Sunday School Superintendent gave my other friend Jean and me a New Testament each. But I never did read it.'

'Where did all this nonsense start? Who put all this rubbish in your head?'

I shrugged. I was just about to start an altercation, seemingly I presumed above her head, outside her religious knowledge, when I saw her eyes rolling ceiling-wards again and she exclaimed impatiently, 'You can't leave religion alone, can you? Thank God *I* haven't had anything to do with all that stuff!'

'Win! Win! Sarah! Stop rowing.'

She got up and thrust open the dining room door.

'What are you up to?' my father asked, lifting his face towards my mother. 'You two can't be together without raising your voices.'

My mother shook her head. 'We weren't rowing.'

The frown slipped from his face and he said bitterly, 'I

7

suppose she thinks she knows everything because of her books and her Bible. She's turned into a snooty big-head.'

Overhearing, I burst into the dining room, ready to put in my two pennyworth, but my mother swung round and, pointing to the door, snapped, 'Out!'

I walked up the stairs, my head shaking; I stomped across the landing and thrust open the door of my bedroom. Mother attempted to follow, but I turned to look, staring hard at her before I cheeked her. 'Don't look at me like that, Mum! You or Dad are being horrid for that matter. If I want to get baptised ... me with the rest of Wimbledon ... then I ... we ... shall.'

'I don't know where you get your nasty ways from.'

'You! Everyone says I'm the spitting image of you.'

After the beginning of the argument the doorbell rang; a few minutes later my mother stared at me, then, looking back at me, she hurried down the stairs. She said, abruptly, 'Wait there! Whoever it is, I'll get rid of them.'

It was perhaps about half a minute before she opened the front door and a short dumpy man, sporting a dark suit and a black thick overcoat, was about to ring the doorbell again.

Neither made any remark at first. Then, in his broad Scottish accent, the man made some courteous comment about the weather and how were both she and the man of the house.

After closing the door, my mother stood aside, having realised who he was. I hurried down the stairs, tidying my hair as I went.

'This is Mr McNicol, Mum.'

It seemed like another full minute before she answered.

'Yes, yes, I've heard about you. By the way, my husband is resting; so, if you don't mind coming through to the breakfast room ...'

I seemed to inwardly know she wanted to spit out her venom, but she also wanted to present her case, yet she

remained quiet and without making a fuss. Even so, he'd made the first move, keeping it to the letter as he explained about the baptism, along with the arrangements, especially as I was still a minor. Both he and my mother paused and looked towards me as if about to speak; yet then changed their minds.

Eventually, as Mr McNicol began to leave, I followed him to the front door. Stopping, he paused to stare at me just as if his brain was experiencing a moment of desolation.

'I had no idea you originated from Jewish stock,' he said before he walked onto the pavement and turned left, heading towards the Baptist church. 'Aren't you the fortunate one!'

'Fortunate! Me?'

On a chilly February evening, wrapped in thick winter clothing, I took a big colourful bath towel from our linen cupboard, and walked the mile or so to South Wimbledon Baptist Church; a place of worship which regrettably no longer exists.

Throughout the baptismal service I sat in the front pew with Christine, a motherly type and a deacon's wife. As the congregation sang the first hymn, 'Take my life and let it be/ consecrated, Lord, to Thee', I slowly turned my head. My eyes swept the congregation to see if Betsy and any of my Christian friends from Westminster Chapel were present, for it had been partly through her I had finally accepted the Lord as my Saviour. They had promised to support me, to witness my baptism. Not one of them came. My eyes filling with tears, I gripped the end of the pew almost to steady myself, as if to still keep hold of my faith somehow.

On my return home, Dad, who wheezed at inconvenient moments, gasped when he saw me, almost as if he'd seen a ghost; he gave me a frightened look. As I attempted to walk in, for a whistle of cold air was blowing into the hall, he tried to stand in my way, giving me an oily smile.

'Hey, Dad, come on; let me in, please!'

He turned slowly, taking his time because of the state of his health. 'So you're back,' he quavered, twisting his neck up out of his open shirt collar.

I think it was Mum who appeared next. 'What ...?' she asked, pointedly, 'What do you think you've been up to? My life!'

Flabbergasted, I squeezed past, telling them both not to be so awful. I wasn't some nasty imp. Mum, followed closely by cousin Sam, who was staying with us for a few days, hurried into the large brown panelled hall. She helped Dad. Icily, his eyes penetrated me. Then, sloping back to the lounge, he groaned: 'How could she? How could she do this to us?' he said repeatedly. 'What is she? Some kind of religious nut?'

My parents were angry; Auntie Maggie, a short blousy woman, disappointed. She later muttered something like, 'See, I told you so,' before exchanging knowing glances with my parents.

Then it happened. The act of Keriah took place, in which the immediate relatives of the deceased tear a portion of their garments, a portion next to their hearts.

The four, all as one, rent their garments, the occasional buttons falling to the floor in front of me, denoting they had not only severed all connections with me, but that in their eyes, I was dead.

A Matzevah, a tombstone, would normally be erected at the Jewish cemetery; it would be erected within one year of their mourning. Had they done that for me? I wondered.

At the beginning of the following week, Lois caught up with me, again calling at my room in the Nurses' Home.

'It's good of you, Lois.'

The remark seemed to hit a nerve. 'Good of me?' She recoiled fastidiously at the very suggestion. 'It wasn't a

question of goodness.'

'So, what did you find; anything?'

'Yeah, but you're probably going to need time to get used to the idea. Oh, Sarah,' she said in a whispered protest. 'Oh, Sarah, it's quite sick.'

I gave a breathy false laugh, which seemed to jump in my throat. 'I think I know what you're going to tell me,' I said, almost defensively, through burning mists welling up in my eyes.

Lois sat bolt upright and bit her lip, rapidly trying to think back. There was a slight tremble in her voice as she said: 'Well now, there's no easy way to tell you ...'

Her mouth fell into a gape and she evidently felt moisture come to her own eyes. This woman who rarely seemed to show emotion, stiffened her body tightly into her waist.

Her hands clutching into her sides, she began again softly. 'Well now, where do I start?'

'Yes, yes, all right. Just get on with it, please. Tell me what exactly happened right from the beginning.'

'Oh, Sarah! All right. Here goes —' Lois thrust a piece of paper towards me, a small tight smile appeared on her face. 'This piece of paper will explain everything.'

Again a silence fell on the room as I read:

Sarah Rebecca Cohen

May, 1946 – February, 1963

I shook my head slowly, swallowed, then glanced up at Lois.

Lois gave a sharp sound in her throat. 'You don't look all that surprised, Sarah. Why not?'

'They're Jews. It's what some Jews do.'

2

The Host of Flowers

On the 8th of June 1940 a marriage was solemnised in Wimbledon between Thomas Henry Cohen and Miss Winifred Violet Jessie Flowers. They first met at the Palais de Danse in Merton; a love quickly grew between the couple, surprising both families, yet causing some misgivings.

To begin with, there was a disparity of fortune. Thomas' father, George Cohen, was only a coal merchant — a man who had died a little after Tom's eighth birthday, leaving few comforts for his family.

His widow, Maude Butler, who scrubbed the steps of Boots the Chemist to earn some money, with three sons and two daughters lived in some austerity at 48 Dundonald Road — a three bedroomed rented property.

The Flowers, however, had made rich pickings from brewing keg bitter. John William Flowers, my maternal grandfather, owned a reasonably handsome, yet terrace house, even so living in some style.

There was a difference, too, in temperament. The Cohens were, on the whole, reserved; the Flowers ardent and outspoken. Indeed the Cohens feared that, in his courtship with Winifred, Tom had abandoned his habitual prudence and acted with impetuosity. The Flowers, for their part, endured

the deepest fears that Win's attachment would end badly, that Tom was only after her forthcoming fortune. The match seemed a troubling enigma. If only Grandfather had wrestled away all impulses to remonstrate with his youngest daughter, for his reservations provoked in her a storm of tears.

So it was, being the satisfied tenants of their home at 86, Haydons Road, South Wimbledon, that Tom and Win mostly lived in some happiness, despite their differences.

Grandfather boasted how he was able to communicate in two languages at the same time. He naturally spoke in his mother tongue of English. However, by using his hands he 'signed'. Being bilingual came naturally to him, his younger brother Frederick and his older sister Violet, because their parents William and Sarah were profoundly deaf, as were Uncles Jack and Edwin, along with their wives Harriet and Anna.

Aunt Anna had a laugh like a donkey, yet never enduring the inconvenience and embarrassment of hearing Frederick mock her with his own attempts at braying laughter.

As a result of such handicaps, it had been tough for the family to find regular and paid employment. In an attempt to combat poverty, they clandestinely brewed beer in the terrace house belonging to John-William and his wife Sarah, storing it on the floor of the cold pantry. Friends and neighbours would come, very often after dark, to purchase the illicit concoction.

A whole pint or jugful rarely cost more than one old penny or two; so the demand grew.

Sarah informed John-William one day how her conscience had the better of her; no longer could she help to trade in an underhand way. She insisted on a business meeting with the rest of the family involved. After several hours of heated debate, Sarah had her own way; they decided to 'come out', openly marketing their beer, showing a healthy profit. By 1880 those investors involved in the business were

able to increase their production, allowing a larger premises to be obtained and valued every worker, from the managers to the old fellow who swept the floors. Everyone was happy.

John and Sarah's finances were able to provide a fine education for their children; something they themselves missed out on. My grandfather started first at a Blue Coat School before moving to a fee-paying school in Westminster, and then on to Oxford's academic seat of learning. However, in 1914 Grandfather, known then as John William Jnr., found himself in the thick of some of the First World War's bloodiest battles.

Peace was restored in 1918. It was about this time that Grandad's maternal aunt, namely the wealthy Kate Mann, made an almost unbeatable offer to buy out the Flowers Brewery. Flowers attempted to resist the takeover by amalgamating with Hamilton Beers. However, it soon came to light how the Hamiltons were in the midst of their own financial difficulties; they were no longer a safe bet.

In 1924 Mann joined forces with the financially strong Crossman Brewery, so the strong Mann and Crossman marched in to buy out Flowers, yet allowing them to still trade under the name of Flowers' Keg Bitter, bringing an unexpected sense of relief to the family.

In 1925 my great-grandparents, John-William and Sarah Flowers, died within months of each other.

John, their eldest son and their favourite, was left £4,250 — a mighty fortune in those days. Fred and Violet both inherited £1,700.

Grandfather used some of his cash to purchase 86 Haydons Road, Wimbledon, previously built by his late father's builders. In the back garden he grew roses which clad the walls, with a melange of pinks blending from palest blush to deepest crimson, all with intoxicating scents.

A widower when I knew him, Grandad desperately missed his wife. She was named Esther, but everyone who

knew her well called her Polly. He met Polly during one of his short holidays in Dublin. Never previously having been out of Ireland, she was a pretty young Jewish girl with a mop of long dark brown curly hair scrunched back into a bun.

As soon as he saw her Irish ice-blue eyes, it was love at first sight. To await her correspondence seemed tiresome. He received her letters with shaking fingers and a thudding heart, missing her more than words can tell. Never one for anything but the briefest of formalities, Grandad came straight to the point, asking Polly's father for his daughter's hand in marriage, promising not only generous sentiments, but shares in the Flowers' fortune as well, sustaining comforts all her days.

Following a fairytale wedding, joined by her younger sister Jessie, Polly found herself to be in charge of the household's arrangements, which rarely intruded into Grandad's life, he regarding that department as much as Polly's as her confinements.

Exactly nine months after their honeymoon, Polly prided herself on producing Eleanor, before a healthy boy named Jack came into the world. All too soon, her physician informed her she would have another child the following spring. After twelve confinements, a tiny little scrap named Winifred Violet Jessie entered the world.

Win, as she was known, was a pale, sickly child, with solemn brown eyes much too large for her delicate face, and invariably caused Grandad to lose patience with Polly: 'You mollycoddle that child,' he'd say with a tiresome regularity, feeling an intrinsic desire to turn back the clock, half regretting her birth. 'You'll make her neurotic!'

Win's fourteen-year-old weaknesses reached the ears of Kate Mann's second cousin, Nell. Her Christian heart went out to the thin teenager. A prim and proper spinster, Nell lived in an elegant house in Islington, a French maid attending her. A courtier, as well as being a dress designer for the rich

and famous, not excluding royalty, Nell had more money than she knew what to do with.

One summer's day, a black cab drew to a halt on the wide cobbled roadway. Not expecting anyone, Polly peeped out from behind the cream lacy curtains. She took a sharp intake of breath. Recognition parted her lips, as she exclaimed it was Miss Mann! Nell was surveying the front façade as if she was contemplating buying the place. Joseph, the youngest and most mischievous of all their sons, was banished up to his room. Polly stopped her sister from baking and, on only the finest of their Sunday best crockery, was she to make dainty little sandwiches and without the crusts.

'I have come to make a serious offer to you and John, Polly,' Nell began. 'Now I'll come straight to the point, for I have a cabby waiting. My proposition concerns that dear child of yours, young Winifred.'

'Win?' asked Grandad. 'What about her?'

'I'd like to adopt her.'

Polly's mouth fell into a gape. 'Adopt her?' she spluttered. 'Adopt Win? Adopt our daughter? Have you taken leave of your senses, Nell?'

The visitor stiffened, sitting bolt upright on a nearby brown overstuffed sofa. She attempted to swallow a second sandwich. 'I have never ... never had the good fortune to marry and bear children of my own — oh, and by the way, where is Winifred? I'd love to see her before I go.'

'Never mind where she is. It's terrible ... there are no words to describe ... some things; some folk are really hard to take. Right now, Nell, you are one of them! ... How *dare* you come to this house, uninvited and, oh, my life! Are you sure you don't want a few boys, too? What about Joseph, eh? He's only in his room and I could call him down, if you like. Oh, but he couldn't be a milliner, could he?'

Nell attempted to ignore Polly's Irish temper, although she felt the heat flooding her face. 'It's just you and John

have had more than your fair share of children and I have none. I believe, if I had dear Winifred I could bring her up as a good Christian. ... I could train her in my profession. Just imagine! Maybe I should give you more time to consider. And I'll ignore your remarks about Joseph ...'

Grandad stood with his back to the black, old fireplace, the hearth now cold, but stacked with some small logs ready for the next winter, and sucked on his Craven 'A' cigarette. Overlooking her remarks about Christianity, he thought Nell's was a good idea, and, touched by her thoughtfulness, thanked her. Polly's hot temper came to the boil, and, hardly your bead-cap and bonnet person, she hissed at John. She then turned to glare at shocked Nell, who almost fainted at Polly's outburst and needed to be revived with smelling salts.

Sighing and tutting under her breath, Nell left the house, trying to set aside her worries about Win. She was helpless. All she could do was pray for the young girl.

And pray she did.

In 1938, at the age of fifteen and a half, Winifred inherited from her own grandfather's will the vast sum of £50; once again, a tidy fortune for those days.

From it, she told me she bought a new dress for her mother, along with a whole new wardrobe of clothing for herself. She had plenty left for a holiday in Brighton. It was Win's first holiday to the coast, her first breath of sea air, which put the roses in her cheeks.

Polly Flowers apparently died from osteoporosis in 1945 — a year prior to my birth.

Her death was naturally a blow to the whole family, but a terrible shock to her doting husband and, for a year or two, he almost became a recluse in his bedroom, claiming he just wanted a bit of peace and quiet. I remember him as a quiet old man, staring into the flickering flames of fire, smoking too heavily, saying very little.

3

The Nazi Menace

In 1939, when Thomas Cohen, my father, was twenty, he had received his call-up papers to serve in the army. He was ordered to report to a training unit based in the old historic city of Winchester.

As part of his basic military training he, along with the other raw recruits, was marched, sometimes at the double, past the dominating statue of Alfred the Great in Broadway, over Bridge Street and up and down Magdalen Hill; all this to kick them into shape as England's fighting men.

'Platoon ... wait fer it ... platoon atten...shun! Right turn ... qui-eek march!' yelled the drill sergeant, his shoulders jerking downwards every time he bellowed yet another command. 'Swing those arms and get into step, Cohen! Left, right ...'

Silently King Alfred, founder of the English nation, stood with sword lifted high, his shield by his side, and looked down on those men who, like himself eleven hundred years before, were prepared to defend this green and pleasant land from its enemies.

King Alfred was not the only observer of all this military activity. Winifred Flowers, hearing that her sweetheart, Tom,

was in Winchester, had immediately decided to holiday there for a week or two so that she could share with him whatever off duty hours he was allowed.

Sitting alone on a park bench, in the shadow of Alfred's statue, she saw it all. Not one to suffer in silence, Winifred observed the strenuous activity and verbal abuse that her love endured at the hands of the non-commissioned officers and decided to take the matter further.

As the Commanding Officer opened his mail he must have roared with laughter at the letter of protest he received from Winifred, who reminded him that she was not a person without influence.

Tom's lot did not noticeably improve!

It was before being posted overseas that he married my Mum. The wedding was a triumph, with many saying it was the best wartime occasion they'd attended.

Father requested leave for the wedding, but at the last moment all leave was cancelled, so he went AWOL from His Majesty's Forces. Neither Mum, nor any of the guests knew about his misdemeanour. The shock was to come later.

Wartime prevented the newlyweds from travelling to exotic places for their honeymoon; they had to be content with borrowing my Uncle Joe's apartment in Wimbledon for a while — but for a much shorter time than planned. At 4:30 A.M. their sleep was disturbed by the thud, thud of heavy army boots marching up the uncarpeted stairs. Unceremoniously the military police, with their peaked caps pulled down low over their eyes, burst through the bedroom door and loudly ordered my half-naked Dad onto his feet. The bewildered young bride, clutching the bedclothes to herself, was left behind as he was whisked away at a sharp pace to a detention centre for military offenders, otherwise known as the "glass house" where, among other punishments, he was made to whitewash sacks of coal.

The regimental sergeant major, chest well out, cap pulled

down, stood before my dad and eyed him up and down. 'Now then, what 'ave we 'ere then?' he asked in a loud voice.

'Private Cohen,' replied my father.

'Private Cohen, SIR!' corrected the RSM in a parade ground shout. 'When you speak to me, you dozy little man, you address me as SIR, do you 'ear me? I said do you 'ear me? First we get 'Itler ... then what do we get? We get you, you 'orrible specimen of 'umanity!'

When Dad was asked his religion the loud RSM looked up and down one of his umpteen lists before eyeing my father again. He shook his head. 'We 'ave no provision for Jews 'ere, no kosher grub, no rabbis, no synagogues; from now on, son, you are Church of England!'

My father stammered in protest, but the RSM would have none of it — any complaints should be addressed to him in triplicate, which meant they would most likely be ignored.

Active service followed. Dad was posted overseas to join the 8th Army in the desert campaign in North Africa. At the end of 1942 he was captured by the Germans. And then the Nazi nightmare followed.

When his captors at the prisoner of war camp realised he was Jewish, arrangements were immediately made to send him to a concentration camp. As he arrived in enemy-occupied Europe, he was bundled with many more prisoners into a filthy, overcrowded railway wagon. There was a sense of terror in their hearts as the train, in total blackout, rumbled through the night.

The train finally screeched to a halt at its destination and he was shoved by the butt of a German rifle out on to the platform: Auschwitz.

At the death camp Dad was stripped of his clothes and issued with prison garb and one thin grey blanket; like nearly

all others he acquired more clothing only when another prisoner died.

One of the older captives was helping with the disembarkation. 'Say you have a trade,' he whispered to Dad.

'But I haven't,' muttered Dad, with a furrowed brow.

'You 'ave now, mate!' he declared, giving him a gentle shove. 'You're a cobbler with me, okay?'

This helpful employment played a part in keeping Dad going, for those without a trade were the earliest to be herded to the gas chambers.

On one occasion my father found grass which had grown in the mud. He ate it quickly before anyone else had the chance. During his time in Auschwitz he witnessed people being shot, gassed, or starved to death. Disease claimed many lives — usually the elderly and the infants were the first to go. Rats, fleas and leeches almost constantly plagued the living. He often thought of escape, but it was never more than a thought. Some guards were recruited from among the Jewish prisoners who, in order to secure their own survival, played a strong part in the destruction of their own people. The interns hated those Jewish traitors even more than they despised the German guards.

On 27th January 1945, a day when Dad was near total collapse, he heard a loud commotion. All the German guards appeared scared stiff. He couldn't understand what was happening. Fearlessly, groups of Jewish prisoners were dropping to their knees, openly blessing God — behaviour previously punishable by death.

The Russian army had arrived! His ordeal was over.

When the camp was liberated, Dad was sent to a British military base in North Wales where he was nursed back to health.

One day there was an unexpected rapping on the front door of our home. Then, whoever it was just kept their finger on the bell ...

'Who on earth could that be?' queried my mother, hurrying through the hall. As she opened the door, her ebony dark eyes widened; she gasped, her hand covering her mouth. Dad stood there with his skinny arms outstretched. Without a moment's thought she threw her arms around him, unable to let him go, tears of joy running down her cheeks. All that mattered to them both was that they were together again — forever.

I was born in 1946, my brother David eight years later in 1954.

The whole family celebrated and congratulated my parents on having a son. David's birth and circumcision were truly marked occasions.

He was circumcised by the Mohel, a specially trained rabbi. I remember when the Mohel arrived; all the men followed him into the main living room, Dad carrying the little baby, whilst the women waited outside in the drawing room.

Mum jumped as she heard the shrill screams of the baby, helpless to comfort him. Still tired from the birth, she buried her head in her lap, covering her ears. One of her sisters-in-law tried to comfort her, but Mum just shook her off.

The door slowly creaked open. There was the Mohel holding out baby David. Mum quickly took hold of him, her precious little bundle, and sat rocking him to and fro until the high-pitched cries turned to just a snuffly whimper.

'Is it not God's blessing that you have such a fine, healthy son, m'dear?' asked the Mohel in a strong Yiddish accent.

She just nodded, smiling through the blur of her tears.

Eight years later she rocked backwards and forwards, but she was in Dad's arms. They sat together as if in a daze as the paediatrician at Great Ormond Street Children's Hospital approached them.

'I'm afraid we could do no more for David. The Hodgkin's Disease was just too advanced. I really am so very sorry,' he said.

David was dead. Dead! They could not believe what they were hearing.

My parents never seemed to recover from the death of my little brother. Their grief was like an open ulcer that would not heal.

4

The Best Days of Your Life?

Carol Smillie interviewed the comedian Jimmy Tarbuck as one of her guests on the BBC television show 'Smillie's People'. Far from being one of my most favourite television characters, I nevertheless pricked up my ears as Mr Tarbuck recollected how one particular schoolteacher constantly made his schooldays miserable. Even when he did excel in a subject the teacher derived pleasure from reminding him of his failures.

Glued by the memories, Mr Tarbuck had obviously carried such hurts from his childhood through into middle age. I felt an empathy. I remembered suffering at the hands of a similar such person for two agonising years way back in the middle 1950s.

At about the age of three I started as an outpatient at Moorfields Eye Hospital in an attempt to correct my squint. Week after week I saw Mr Cross, an eminent ophthalmic surgeon, although the consultations were getting me nowhere.

Grandfather, who had little or no medical knowledge, decided he'd had enough of the airy-fairy theories and went to

see the consultant himself.

'I am John Flowers,' he began.

Mr Cross nodded. 'How may I help you?'

'Well, I want something done about my granddaughter's sight ... but if it's a question of money ... no problem, just name the amount, please.'

Mr Cross wasn't interested in any payments, but, even so I was admitted the following week for surgery on one eye and, some two or three years later, the other eye was operated on.

Those were comparatively unenlightened days when any form of hospitalisation separated babies and children from their relatives or friends who might visit.

Frightened, I was undressed and lifted into a bed where cot sides were in situ, just as if I were a baby. Nothing having been explained to me, I was returned from the operating theatre with my eye covered, the white cotton patch held in place by a crepe bandage wound round my head. There was no one to kiss me goodnight, say my prayers with me, or read me a bed-time story from one of my favourite books; just one very gruff nurse who spanked me on my right forearm for not being able to swallow my pre-med tablets all in one go. Why the tablets couldn't have been crushed, or I could not have been given the pre-med in liquid form is beyond me.

I can still remember those awful days when my sight was either blurred or I had double vision. Ophthalmic surgery at that time had a long way to go.

Jessie Taylor, my cousin's wife, said I had arrived at Moorfields with pretty ribbons in my hair, and left with a patch over my eye, kept in place by a frayed cotton bandage.

My then teacher was the compassionate Mrs Hughes who made allowances for me, moving me to the front of the class, enabling me to see the blackboard without much difficulty, she constantly spurring me on with the delights of learning.

During the following academic year I found myself in All

Saints Junior School where Miss White was my teacher; and Mr Baxter was then the Headmaster.

'Find yourself a seat,' she instructed, confronting the jumble of young faces on the first day of term. 'Come on! Hurry up, the lot of you.'

I attempted to sit at the front, but the overbearing Joyce, a local greengrocer's child and her faithful friend, Judith, had hogged those seats. I was left standing, searching for an empty desk nearer the blackboard.

Miss White sighed. 'What's the matter with you?' she enquired in her penetrating and abrupt voice. 'Yes ... yes, you girl ... you with the glasses.'

I'd never been addressed as "the girl with the glasses" before. I scowled, for she too had glasses — hexagonal rimless ones. I longed to say something in retaliation, but I had been taught to always be polite. Teachers, policemen, parents; in fact, towards all grown-ups I was courteous.

'I'm sorry, Miss, but I need to be at the front,' I replied nervously. 'I can't see well if I'm seated at the back of the class.'

'Well, tough! There are only seats at the back ... go on. So, go on then — don't just stand there like a lemon.'

'Couldn't someone just change seats with me, please?'

She turned to those rooted at the front. 'Do any of you want to change with her?' she asked.

Not one child moved. Then Judith began to vacate her seat, but Joyce yanked the girl's sleeve and she sat down.

'Well, little Miss Specky Four Eyes, it looks as if you are remaining at the back, doesn't it?'

Several children chuckled at the insulting name she had for me, especially Joyce, the tall, plump girl who happily bullied anyone weaker.

'I beg your pardon, but my name is Sarah, Sarah Cohen; nothing else. Not Miss Specky Four Eyes!'

An irritated Miss White, probably only in her middle

twenties, soon to be married to a Scot, turned red in the face. She hadn't bargained on this response. Not from the likes of me.

Previously I excelled at school, never lower than the top two or three; but now I was failing miserably. I could not see what was chalked up on the blackboard so, eventually, I just didn't bother.

'You, come out here,' shot Miss White. 'Come out here right now, you stupid girl.'

Fearfully, I made my way to her desk. She picked up a twelve-inch wooden ruler and hit my left bare forearm until the weapon nearly snapped in two. 'That's for looking out of the window instead of working,' she smirked, apparently pleased to have administered the punishment. 'Now go back to your desk and pay attention in future. Do you hear? You're a dense, useless girl and someone like you will never get to be anything more than some sort of factory girl ... if that.'

Mr Baxter was made aware of my lack of commitment concerning the schoolwork. 'All she does is stare out of the window,' he explained to my worried father. 'Maybe you should think about sending her to a special school for the not very bright.'

Dad shook his head. 'But she used to do so well. She was a clever girl.'

After supper Dad sat me down beside him and asked why I no longer took much interest at school. Between my choking sobs and showing him my sore reddened arm, I explained. It was one of the rare occasions when he boiled over with rage. 'How dare she do this to you!' he yelled. 'How *dare* she? And I'll be having words with Joyce's dad, too.'

The next day he and my mother, supported by my doting grandad, a strong-willed man who loved me to bits, warned the teacher concerning her actions. For a short time, running

maybe into a couple of weeks, Miss White attempted to change her attitude; but it didn't last. She was soon back to her old self, rulering me as often as possible.

'I'll always get the better of you,' she barked at me.

When I told my grandfather things were worsening, he and my parents enquired about sending me to a fee-paying boarding school, well known for its small classes and high standards of academic and sporting achievements — swimming in particular.

After about five years of being a weekly boarder, I began to meet up on a Saturday evening with a teenage group. Many of us, mostly all Jewish, had been friends for years. Most of our parents were friends too, mainly through the Jewish community events which took place in and around the synagogue in Worple Road, Wimbledon.

We Jewish children growing up in the fifties and sixties were, on the whole, obedient to our parents. However, when I was about sixteen, I'd briefly met the eldest brother of one of my Gentile friends; he was at least eight years my senior, drop-dead gorgeous and owned a bright red sports car.

This young man had accompanied a small group of us to see the play "Arsenic and Old Lace" at the Wimbledon Theatre. His seat was next to mine, and during the interval he and I chatted and eventually he asked me to have a meal with him.

'We're going to a restaurant,' I informed my parents the next day.

'Oh yes, and who else will be there?' asked my dad.

'Just us,' I replied.

'What? Just you and him? No chaperone?'

I nodded.

'And how are you going to get to this restaurant, eh?'

'He has a brand new red sports car ...'

'So how old is this fellow?'

I shrugged.

'Sarah, you must have a rough idea.'

'I dunno. Perhaps about twenty-four — '

'Or he could be older, huh?' interrupted my mother. 'He's too old for you; and what's this Jew's name?'

'Andy.'

'Andy?' quizzed my dad. 'Andy isn't exactly Jewish, is it? Right. That does it. You're not going out with this man ... a Gentile with more money than sense who is too old for you ... and that's that.'

'I'm going out for a meal. That's all.'

'You're not going, Sarah.'

'Dad, I am.'

My dad was a little more than annoyed.

The day of the date arrived and, having made myself up to look older than my years, I rushed out of the house and into the passenger seat of Andy's red sports car.

During my absence Dad decided to teach me a lesson.

After the meal the drop-dead gorgeous Andy drove me home. He jumped out of his car and escorted me from the passenger seat. He was just about to kiss me goodnight when my dad opened a bedroom window and shouted: 'Ethel! Come on in! Your mother's waiting to bath you!'

Andy was flabbergasted. 'Ethel? Why did he call you Ethel? I thought your name was Sarah, and surely she doesn't still bath you ...'

With that, he drove off at speed and I never saw him again. However, I fled into the house and tore up the stairs to my dad, who thought what he'd done was absolutely hilarious.

Humiliated to the core, it was probably at least a month before I would even speak to my dad who had got his own way, stopping me from dating an older Gentile against his will.

We teenagers usually met up in the Orinoco Coffee shop and chatted for what seemed ages over a cup of frothy, espresso coffee, discussing evocative subjects such as politics and religion.

Constantly confused concerning the existence of God, I would listen carefully to what the others in the group had to say about a Supreme Being. After a while, I secretly tried to please Him, if He existed at all, by attempting to measure up to the standards set by the Ten Commandments. The religious guideposts made morality a fairly uncomplicated business, as they clearly assessed my conduct as either good or bad. Surely, if I lived a good life, then this God might be pleased with me.

Sin, I understood, was a failure to live up to God's standard, but the way some Roman Catholics handled their moral failures differed greatly from the way I had to cope. They did not seem to take failure too seriously, but went to the confessional twice a year, got it off their chests and invariably carried on much as before. The Day of Atonement, which takes place in the autumn of each year, is when Jews repent of their sins and seek forgiveness. I seemed to repress my guilt and constantly carry it about with me.

I did wonder if God might be found in other religions, but this was most certainly discouraged by my family. In those days, people were not encouraged to investigate other faiths. One of the old nuns who taught religion to the girls in my school warned their own girls against investigating Judaism. She said if they adopted it, it would be a horrible sin; appropriate punishments would follow. My friend, Susan, made a comment about Jesus, Mary and Joseph being of my Jewish religion. She was sent to the Mistress of Discipline and rapidly silenced.

Chatting with some Upper Sixth Formers, who were obviously more sophisticated than any of the girls in my age group, I realised they seemed to be moving away from the

religion of their childhood. Some had travelled to exotic places, experienced various cultures and acquired a tolerance for other people's customs. They had begun to explore their own sexuality in a less puritanical way, and were throwing off the constraints of their religious upbringing. What they had to say was fascinating, yet of no help in my search for God.

Normally I felt very Jewish; at other times I felt myself to be something else. What I was sure of was my need to find something or someone to believe in. I felt that there must be a power behind the universe; there must be a meaning for my life here on earth, and beyond into eternity. If there was anyone up there, then why didn't He manifest Himself to me?

Strolling through the school's garden I picked one of the roses. I stood for a moment or two stroking the softness of the pink petals; not even the finest of scientists could even begin to make such a lovely thing. So, the God whom I was seeking must surely be responsible for the creation all around me.

Later that afternoon, just after tea, I wandered into a little chapel. The smell of stale incense was pervading the place. Staring up at the large wooden cross hanging above the altar, I whispered: 'Are you there, O Supreme Being? If you really do exist, then I am here. Please, are you able to make yourself known to me?'

One of the nuns, an Irish woman, came quietly into the chapel. She was quite surprised to find me, of all people, kneeling in one of the pews. After genuflecting, she knelt beside me; she felt too close. I felt irritated that she was invading my personal space, stopping my train of thought.

'Are you all right?' she asked. 'May I help you in some way?'

I shook my head and sighed at her. Taking the hint, she moved to the back of the chapel, tidied up a pile of hymnbooks, gave a bob a little in the direction of the altar and left.

31

Alone again, my mind wandered, almost forgetting why I was there. I left and returned to my study bedroom.

During the following weekend time seemed to drag for me, so I decided I would talk to my parents about one of the teachers at my school. She was an active member at Westminster Chapel. She'd told me how she had become a Christian during her student days at the Philippa Faucet College. She had also asked me if I'd like to join her one Sunday, to attend a service at Westminster Chapel.

'My life! You want to do what?' Grandfather queried. 'A church ... a Christian church? Whatever for?'

Mum made her way into the room. 'Are you upsetting your grandad?' she questioned. 'What have you been saying to him, huh?'

'I only said I wanted to go to Westminster Chapel; that's all.'

'What do you mean "that's all"? What on earth do you want to go there for, huh?'

Grandad rocked backwards and forwards in his chair. 'Mark my words, she'll become some sort of Christian nut if she gets involved with her. I've heard about these zealous evangelical crackpots.'

'Be quiet, Dad,' she snapped. 'Sarah won't do anything of the kind. And that's that.' Mother shushed at her father, determined she would settle the matter with me.

'Have you taken leave of your senses? I'm telling you, no one else but me,' she continued. 'I'm telling you that you'll be mad to go,' she declared. 'Listen to me, Sarah, you are a Jewish girl ... don't get involved with this teacher. She's old enough to be your mother, and I don't want to hear another thing about Christian churches. Okay?'

So I went.

The next Sunday I hurried to meet Betsy, my maths teacher, outside London's Victoria railway station. I was early; twenty minutes early and I had to hang around as the

fine drizzle was falling and the whole of the West End of London seemed cloaked with crystal-tipped gloom. When she arrived, neat and respectably dressed, we strode jauntily through Stag Place and along to Westminster Chapel in Buckingham Gate.

I sat up in the balcony with her, directly facing the pulpit. I wondered how on earth two thousand people could sit motionless, in complete silence, with all eyes glued on the Welshman in the Geneva gown as he stood to preach with an authority everyone seemed to accept. All this was in stark contrast to synagogue worship, where one is free to move around at will and chat.

When the service was over, the length of which came as quite a shock to me, those staying for the day scurried off to rescue their jacket potatoes from the church's hot ovens; every Sunday a basic lunch was consumed by the members who'd travelled from far and wide. The conversation along the trestle tables was mostly about the hour's sermon. Feeling like a spare part, I sat examining a crease in the white tablecloth, trying to appear as bright as those around me, all skilfully untangling Christian knots with their Biblical knowledge.

Filled with a momentary wave of dismay, I had not realised when I accepted Betsy's invitation, that it was to be a full day's programme! After the lunch, which was nothing like my mother's huge Sunday roasts, Betsy and her friends took a circular walk around St James's Park, with me trailing, before assembling with the other women in one of the church rooms for a Bible study. Most of the women of indeterminate years seemed to me very old, as did most people over thirty!

Tea and sandwiches followed. A prayer meeting led up to the evening service which for me, as an unimpressed non-Christian teenager, was no better than the morning act of worship. This preceded a time of fellowship, when those people whom I regarded as congenitally incapable of doing

anything wrong, stood around in groups, drinking coffee and talking about such things as when they were born-again, leaving me even more like the proverbial fish out of water; very much the awkward pupil of the thirty-one year old serious teacher with the still face. I could not see what all the fuss was about, catapulting me into a state of religious doubt. I was glad to return home!

'Well, Sarah, I suppose you hated being with that teacher woman, eh?' asked my dad, peering from behind his Sunday newspaper. He was a man of temperate, even indifferent, belief himself, and he deplored any fervent expression showing up in me. On the whole he enjoyed synagogue life, but he had not grown into it because of any overwhelming religious conviction. He'd just been born into it, and that was that.

Gathering myself into a puffed-up self-importance, I stood bolt upright. 'No, I didn't hate it,' I stated, not prepared to admit defeat. 'It was smashing and I'm going again next week!'

I repeated the morning services, lunches, walks, Bible studies, teas, evening worship and fellowship time for Sunday after Sunday. My parents suspected that I was only going to Westminster Chapel out of sheer rebellion, but Betsy encouraged me to attend every week. She even bought me a Bible. Not knowing what to do with it, I began to flick through the pages at random. It opened at Isaiah, Chapter 53.

Knowing only a very little Old Testament scripture, I remembered an old rabbi once preaching from this passage. He claimed it only referred to the suffering servant Israel; absolutely nothing to do with Jesus. I wondered, as I read through the entire chapter, whether or not he'd been mistaken; maybe this was indeed about Jesus and maybe He was the Messiah. The Christians, just like the nun, Sister Helen Curmi in St Anthony's Hospital, claimed that Jesus was the Messiah. He was their Messiah, too, their Christ, the

Anointed One who'd apparently fulfilled all the Old Testament Scripture.

'Who has believed our message?' verse one of the 53rd Chapter asked.

'But why should I, Lord? I'm a well-bred kind of girl, from a good family, educated at a good school, and clearly knowing all the right people.' It was ridiculous to worry out of hand that I was bad, yet I still felt no better, just full of murky gloom; like a lesser mortal valiantly struggling not to wilt. Knowing I was an unbeliever, a momentary wave of terror was borne in upon me; I suddenly wanted to trust Him, commit myself to Him, and go to heaven when I die. Betsy had told me that if I didn't trust in the Lord Jesus, then I'd go to hell. Hell? Oh, no! I was scared stiff.

Without more ado I read on further until I had completed the entire chapter.

Then I began to read it over and over again, homing in on the third verse. *'He was despised and rejected by men.'*

Had I despised and rejected Him?

However, although I expected something amazing to happen, I returned home that evening not feeling any different.

The following Sunday I was preparing to attend Westminster Chapel and I was on my way to Wimbledon railway station when I was stopped by a black car. Betsy was the driver. I thought, at first, she was stopping to give me a lift and attempted to hurry around to the passenger seat, but Mike, her youngest brother, already occupied it. Her parents were in the back.

'Sorry,' she said, with a grin, 'but I already have a car full.'

'It's okay. I'll catch the train.'

'Right. See you there, then.'

Watching her drive off, I changed my plans and walked back towards South Wimbledon Methodist Church. I crept in

just as the choir were about to start up. I decided to attend the evening service, too, for I had already met the minister once or twice — then the Rev. John Clifford. He was the large fatherly type who had invited me to attend a service while I was in St. Anthony's Hospital when I had appendicitis. He was one of the hospital chaplains.

When he visited me then, he had told me about John Wesley's conversion. John Wesley went unwillingly to a society in Aldersgate Street where Luther's preface to the Epistle to the Romans was being preached on. About a quarter to nine, while the preacher was describing the change which God works in the heart through faith in Christ, he felt his heart strangely warmed. Wesley then trusted in Christ, Christ alone, for salvation; assurance was given for that. Christ had taken away his sins, even his, and saved him from the law of sin and death.

That happened within the eighteenth century to John Wesley, but there I was, seated in a pew in a Methodist church, virtually ignoring the rest of the congregation all around me, praying with all my might that Christ would come into my life once and for all — that He would 'strangely warm' my heart, giving me salvation. The Lord did just as I'd pleaded, for, just as I opened my eyes I turned to see the large old clock at the back of the church. It showed seven twenty-two ... the time of *my* heart being 'strangely warmed', just like John Wesley's.

The following Thursday I called in at Mr Clifford's vestry.

'I saw your sign outside which said, "A trouble shared is a trouble halved",' I told him.

He smiled. 'Sit down, my dear. Tell me, what's your trouble?'

I shook my head and beamed. 'I don't have a trouble really. I wanted to tell you what happened to me on Sunday evening.'

When I told him how Christ became real to me, he exclaimed:

'Well, well, well. That's some experience, eh?'

I agreed, still feeling the wonder of it.

'And so, m'dear, shall you start to come here regularly then?'

Shaking my head, I told him I would continue to attend Westminster Chapel.

He grinned a knowing sort of grin. 'Well, if you go there you'll need to always take a Bible with you.'

'I think I shall.'

Mr Clifford asked me how my parents were dealing with my new-found faith, with my future attendance being at Westminster Chapel.

It was not an easy question to answer.

5

Farewell Leonardo

Having spent several hours immersed in the Scriptures, starting with St John's Gospel in particular, I wanted to be nothing more now than a receptacle of the sleep of the just, unconscious, totally submitted to the night; yet sleep eluded me. Hoisting myself up on one elbow and squinting through into the darkness, I fumbled to once again switch on my small bedside lamp, immediately bathing the cosy, square bedroom into pools of dazzling brilliance. I groped for the alarm clock. Shaking the unreliable timepiece, I grimaced, breathing forcefully from behind my teeth; the wretched contraption had stopped again and it would never get me up in the morning.

Throwing back the duvet, I slipped my feet from the warm bed and, shivering involuntarily, stretched across to the wicker armchair where my dressing gown, the one which flapped around my ankles when I walked, had been lazily thrown the night before. Parting the pink floral curtains just a little, which fell in ample folds to the floor, I gazed out into the haunting stillness. At that moment the full moon made a brief appearance from behind a passing cloud, dancing in fragments through the gaps between the branches of a huge withered-up old tree; it was just possible, but by squinting

hard, I could just see the local parish church's illuminated clock under different stars. It was a little after one-thirty.

Mum, having paid a nocturnal visit to the bathroom, was immediately sensitive to my movements.

'Yoo-hoo, Sarah, are you all right?' she called through in a loud whisper, straining hard to catch any sounds of betraying activities from within. 'Would it be okay for me to come in?'

I reeled rapidly, almost in stumbling orbit, back into bed, dressing gown and all, half-feigning sleep.

She put her head around my door. 'Oh, sorry,' she said, crestfallen, her dark eyes straying in. 'I didn't mean to wake you. It's just that — well, I thought I heard you ...'

Camouflaged under the bulky bedding, I faked a lazy yawn. 'It's okay. You'd better come in.'

'Hmm. I suppose you can't sleep because of this crazy decision of yours, eh?' Mum remarked, her mind knitting away with speculation, forced to no other conclusion. 'Leaving Art College ... honestly, I really think you've taken leave of your senses.'

Suddenly, she had one of her blinding flashes. 'Hey, I won't be long — I'll fetch us some camomile tea. That'll help us both to sleep ... it makes all the difference in the world, does a nice cup of tea.'

'Mum, please, I don't want any. I really don't like it.'

Her eyes narrowed fractionally into slits as she pointed one index finger. 'Of course y' do! Now I'll be back in just a jiffy,' she declared, not prepared to negotiate.

Effortlessly, like a sprinter getting off his block, she darted down the stairs to the little hall and then into the kitchen where she plugged in the kettle, dropping tea leaves into the pot.

Sitting up in bed, my chin on my chest, tightly hugging my knees under the bedding, I groaned with a sense of foreboding: how my mother's 'all girls together cuppa' would

mean a long oration concerning my future, haranguing me on the foolhardiness of listening to Christians, Dorothy, Betsy's best friend, in particular; of suddenly quitting Art College. Then she'd most likely progress on to the 'Have you forgotten the sacrifices Daddy and I made for you to go to college in the first place?' scenario, as if money was a big problem for them, she being a beneficiary of the Flowers breweries! Oh, it was the wrong time for such weightier topics of conversation, yet she'd still do what she was determined to do.

Moments later, Mum, pushing my creaking bedroom door open, emerged with a tray of the medicinal beverage to be imbibed.

It wasn't long before the old familiar pattern set in. 'I remember ...' began Mother, with a surging ocean of vivid memories, 'I remember when I was a teenager, how I got crazy thoughts into my head, but ... oh ... never, never daft ideas about Christianity. And I certainly never got involved with old spinsters old enough to be my parents.'

I sighed, taking a long swallow.

'But there, it'll probably only be a nine-day wonder, just like your pop stars and the peace movement — that CND movement.'

Oh, why couldn't she have gone back to bed, or been robbed of her power of speech? Only for a while, not forever — just that night, I thought.

'No, Sarah, I've told Daddy not to worry — you'll be over it all soon. We just need to be patient. You'll be back to your old self before long. Maybe you can enrol again in the Art School when you are thinking straight.'

As a student on the foundation course at the Wimbledon College of Art and Design, I had excelled. Part of the course was the life class. Betsy's closest friend, Dorothy, an only child of elderly parents and a drab secretary in her thirties, was 'old' for her years, maybe through the sheltered life led

so far. It was she who'd told me I should give up Art College. On enquiring why, she, referring to the life classes, which were a vital part of the course, informed me I was nothing more than a budding 'pornographer'! I couldn't have been more offended ... shocked even. I wondered how she'd come to that conclusion.

'What if your drawings got into the wrong hands?' she asked, with a frown. 'Your work may well encourage unhealthy sexual thoughts ... and you now claiming to be a Christian, too! You can't live the sort of life you lived before becoming a Christian.'

I wanted to retaliate, explaining how my pencil work only showed line and form, light and shade. Nevertheless, I was still a very new believer, young for my seventeen years, and incredibly impressionable, desperately longing to do the right thing in the sight of the Lord Jesus Christ. Believing that the older, mature Christians had to hold in their grasp all the right answers, it was to them, my spiritual props, I came.

Listening to Dorothy's words, instead of making up my own mind, I abandoned the college course, wanting my new-found faith to grow, to be uppermost and solid.

Although during the early sixties there were still those like Dorothy, who discouraged participation in drama, art and entertainment, there were others who questioned the rigid division of life into sacred and secular. In my Jewish and cultural background, based on the Old Testament, the whole of life was seen to be important and God given. One of the Jewish rabbinical writings states: 'A man will have to give an account on Judgement Day of every good thing he could have enjoyed and didn't'!

There were many in the Church of those days who curtailed their activities, not because the Spirit of God had convicted them of wrongdoing, but because they were afraid of disapproval, of what their Christian friends might think of them if they ventured outside the constricted lifestyle: no

theatre, no cinema, no dancing. Nothing.

On the British musical scene it was not really until Cliff (now Sir Cliff) Richard, performing in show business, took a stand as a Christian believer, and began to break the mould.

However, some evangelical churches seemed to think those with any sort of artistic talent were only there to do posters! One church minister asked me to design and paint a poster. It regrettably created some hilarity from the congregation, but caused him, and definitely me, some embarrassment, for it read:

THE MINISTER WILL BE PLEASED TO SEE ANY VISITORS TO THE CHURCH IN HIS VESTY AFTER THE SERVICE.

When I was really quite young, maybe only about five or six, my father took me along to the Latimer Road swimming pool late one Sunday morning and, when I didn't immediately turn into an Olympic gold medallist there and then, he muttered on for the rest of the day. 'If she just did exactly as I said ... if she'd trust me ... if she'd just have realised she wasn't going to drown ... that the water would hold her up, that I'd hold her up ...'

Oh, and then there was the bright red two-wheeler bike, which was much too big and heavy for me. 'If she'd just do as I told her,' he yelled. 'She has no idea of balance! She turns the handlebars in the wrong direction and wonders why she falls off — don't blame me for the cut on her knee for, before I knew it, she was in the gravel.'

He planned to teach me to drive!

'Dad,' I began, a worried look across my brow, 'may I have proper lessons with a school of motoring? I think I'd do better with a real instructor.'

'An instructor? What can an instructor teach you that I can't?'

'Well, he might be a little more patient, don't you think?'

'What d'yer mean "more patient", eh? I'm always patient!'

I shrugged, staring in the direction of my mother, hoping for her support, but she had that distant, far away look which really said it all — it said: 'leave me out of it'.

That morning Dad marched me out and, seating me behind the wheel of his old black Ford he, for about the first time ever, was the nervous passenger in the seat where one has a different view of the road and the oncoming traffic.

After I kangarooed the car along the first few yards, Dad raised his eyes heavenwards and sighed, fingers drumming on his knee.

'Steer it straight; no, put your left foot right down on the clutch before changing gear ... my life, at this rate I'll need a new gearbox! No, no, not crunching it like that ... mind that bus! What d'yer mean "which bus?" You'll kill that cyclist if you're not more careful. Mind! Look out! Slow down! That's it ... that's it ... that's enough! I'll drive us home.'

My mother stared up at us from where she was sitting on the sofa. 'My, you're both home sooner than I'd expected,' she said with surprise.

'Home?' boomed my father. 'It's a wonder we are home at all. It's a miracle we're not both in St Helier's Hospital mortuary.'

'Now, now, dear, don't exaggerate.'

'Exaggerate? I'm not exaggerating. She nearly killed a cyclist and then, when I said, "Mind the bus" do you know what she said?'

Mum shook her head, showing little or no interest.

'I'll tell you what she said — she asked: "What bus?" What bus indeed! How can you not see a great big red London bus in front of you? She'd be safer behind a last World War machine gun than a wheel. Heavens, a car is just as much a lethal weapon as ...'

Mum smiled in my direction and, seeing I was near to tears, told him to be quiet.

'Don't tell me to be quiet. I tell you I was safer in front of Rommel's lot during the last war than I was with her today.'

'All he did was shout,' I began, attempting to get in my two pennyworth. 'I've never been in the driver's seat before and he virtually expected me to be ready for a Grand Prix. Shout, shout, shout! How can I learn anything when he's constantly yelling all the time? He makes me all of a dither.'

Dad attempted to open his mouth again, but this time it was Mum who did the talking. 'If you weren't so tight fisted you'd have *paid* for her to learn to drive,' she snapped, scowling hard at him.

'Tight fisted? Me? Tight fisted! That's the last thing I am — in fact, my middle name should be Money Bags!'

The next day it was Mum who, with Dad's money, paid for me to have twenty lessons with the British School of Motoring.

'She'll need more than twenty,' sniped Dad. 'More like two hundred and twenty!'

Soon it was the big day, the day of my test. An hour before coming face to face with the examiner I had my final lesson. 'You'll do fine,' said my driving instructor. 'Don't be nervous — take a deep breath and drive for him as you have for me. Okay?'

The examiner was as po-faced as I'd half expected, but that wasn't my main problem. It was Dad! Everywhere I went, he followed. His car was constantly on my tail — all I saw in my mirror was his Ford. When I did the expected three-point turn, he being parked a little way away gave me the thumbs up.

'And what do you think you were playing at, Dad?' I demanded, banging through the house like a Nazi storm-trooper. 'Why were you following me?'

'Because you were in the car with an entirely strange

man, for goodness' sake. How would I know whether or not you were safe?'

'He was the examiner! What harm would I have come to with him, eh? You could have unnerved me so much that I might have failed.'

'But you didn't, did you?' he beamed.

And then a thought struck him. 'I hope you don't think you are now going to borrow my car to go swanning off up to that Westminster church ...'

'Chapel,' I corrected. 'It's known as Westminster Chapel.'

'Whatever. You're definitely not borrowing my car to go to any Christian church, okay? If you insist on giving up your Art College course to go and work in a dusty old library, and irritating us by going to church, then you can jolly well find the money to travel by the train.'

Oh, I didn't know how to get through the following week without exploding, for life seemed to be closing in on me from all sides. I quite enjoyed my working days in the library and, in a way, looked upon it as an escape from the household. Until two and a half weeks previously, when I had given my senior tutor, whose name I forget, a definite 'no' to my course at Wimbledon College of Art and Design. He had raised his voice, coming back at me with, 'What a waste!'

Stressed, for the first time in our acquaintance, the chief Librarian couldn't understand why I was to work for him in Battersea Public Library when I eventually planned to enter nursing.

'As a stopgap. The library is to be a stopgap.'

'Not the nurse's uniform then, eh? You're not just swayed by the romance of it all then?'

'I'm a Christian and one of our church members thinks the life classes at Art School are nothing but ... but porn,' I replied, daring to stand up to him. 'So you see, I have no choice.'

His frozen look, previously suppressed, became all too visible as he retorted stiffly, 'I think you're a bit of a fool and you've listened to a fool. And what does that Christian know about life classes? Anyway, if you want to work here, I'll employ you as a shelf stacker until you go into nursing. Okay?'

6

Hammersmith the Mecca of Medicine!

My first impressions of Hammersmith Hospital were not unfavourable. Most of the students on our first day, way back in the September of 1964, were quiet women.

One or two were outstanding and seemed to already know their way around; they were postgraduates who were already qualified as psychiatric nurses.

Those were also the days of Bishop John Robinson and the Bishop of Durham, who were leading some to question the virgin birth and the resurrection of Christ. Not I.

For me, the Cross of the Lord Jesus was a once-for-all atoning death. I was a staunch conservative evangelical who would never deny the virgin birth and the resurrection.

The first three months were spent at a preliminary training school in Ealing under a noble-looking tutor. Miss Porter's thrust of lectures made sure we were all up at an early hour each morning, believing she could make us into brilliant nurses — the best in the world!

Shortly after we left the desks and Miss Porter's academic and insensitive lectures, with our weekends free, we were confronted by a notice on the board one day, to the effect that

all of us would be required to pack and live in at the hospital.

'You'll find another notice board in the Nurses' Home which will tell you the ward to which you'll be allocated,' she explained in her broad Lancashire accent. 'And remember, none of you is "God's gift to Nursing". Right? Good!'

The thrust of her lectures seemed to go to naught once we were on our way to being let loose on the poor, unsuspecting patients, as our tutor had said to us; probably also to every fresh set of future nurses. They will all have heard the same.

Installed in my room, not only did I find myself being 'looked after' by an Irish Home Sister, but I was sharing with Oakley — a bubbly student who became a lifelong chum and was a girl born to nurse, which was all she wanted at the time.

During those nursing days my working life had become the result of circumstances. I had grown up believing I would do something with art because I excelled in it, and I would proceed to take advantage of opportunities, maybe in teaching or commercial art. I wouldn't have minded even being a portrait painter, for, to be fair, I had talent.

However, nursing seemed to choose me. Now I was working within the field of sciences, which was pushing me to open my mind. I was exploring interesting people and varied opportunities and possibilities, nearer and nearer into some sort of Christian work, here or overseas. Who knows?

However, until I'd given this nursing thing a whirl, I couldn't know for sure if, like Oakley, I had a strong bent towards caring for others with all their bodily functions and smells!

After my first ward, a men's medical, I did wonder if I was ill suited for being constantly around sickness and suffering, investing in being something I didn't want to be.

Could I be for years in this profession I disliked, or be with those who didn't like me, to be positive in the face of such a dilemma? Even so, I was no quitter.

Someone — and I can no longer remember who — sent

me a wonderful philosophical statement, and which is sometimes called 'The Serenity Prayer.'

> God, grant me the serenity to accept
> the things I cannot change;
> the courage to change the things I can;
> and the wisdom to know the difference.

So I planned to see my three years of training to its end, and beyond — maybe.

Some parts of my training I hated; and I do not use the word 'hated' lightly! There were many dark days when I could have felt trapped if I hadn't kept my dream of working maybe overseas ahead of me, reminding myself that these three years were simply a part of my life and not the whole of it.

During my time prior to entering nursing I had met some eccentric folk; some relatives, school teachers, church members — all had a little share of either potentially becoming, or had already become crazy. However, some of the nursing sisters, in particular, were not exactly in harmony with the 'normal', whatever normal may be.

One such nursing sister entered the School of Nursing as a tutor and, when her cat encountered a road traffic accident, she catheterised him. Wow! What a sight to see the old moggy walking around the School of Nursing, dragging a catheter.

Another Ward Sister used to wash her knickers out in benzalkonium chloride.

Her colleague couldn't understand why bottles of milk were disappearing, considering she'd chained up the crate!

As students we usually spent six weeks on each ward or speciality. There were some wards I really didn't like. However I adored the children's ward — the babies in particular. I also enjoyed the Intensive Care Unit and I was

good at that, so much so that the Sister asked if I'd work there after my finals. But I didn't.

During the latter part of my training we could choose where we'd like to go — we could go either to St Mark's Hospital or to the Bethlam Psychiatric Hospital. I chose the latter and was allocated to the Boys' Adolescent Ward. I loved every part of my time there until I was kicked — hard.

It started when a few of the qualified staff took some of the boys to a local funfair. One of the lads believed his hand to be his 'bird'. I liked this lad and stayed with him during the time at the fair. On the way back, to prevent him from running into the road, I grabbed hold of his hand. Thinking I was taking his bird, he kicked me so hard on my right shin that I needed to be admitted to Sick Bay to have a haematoma drained.

Three weeks before my finals I spent some time on one of the medical wards. The Sister despised me from her innermost being. At the end of the three weeks I had some leave due. I was about to celebrate my 21st birthday and was off duty for a happy couple of weeks.

'I'm glad you're going, nurse,' she said. 'You're one of the worst students I have ever met. Good riddance to bad rubbish!'

I shrugged. I didn't like her over much.

'Thank goodness I'll never have to see you again,' she declared with a deep scowl.

'Oh, but Sister, I have to come back and work here for another three weeks, to complete my six weeks.'

She muttered something awful and then hurried after a young doctor who was about to take some blood from one of her patients.

'How dare he come in my ward and take blood when it's coming up lunchtime? I'll have *his* blood,' she breathed.

After my twenty-first was over I returned to complete my further time and came face to face with that old Sister.

Although I believed she would start all over again, breathing fire at me, she greeted me with a smile, swearing she'd never seen me before in her life! And what a wonderful nurse I was!

During my three years at this prestigious London Hospital I became part of the Inter-Hospitals Nurses' Christian Fellowship. We met on a Tuesday evening, if we could get the time off. Sometimes we'd gather around the Word of God; other times we'd invite visiting speakers. Occasionally Oakley and I opened our room for prayer.

How I valued those times, finding them both uplifting and inspiring; I grew spiritually.

Sadly, following several upsets and dark tragedies there were two doctors and, I believe, more than a couple of nurses who committed suicide. Another few required psychiatric help, causing some Christians to disappear from the scene.

Others who had been taken in by the late Bishop of Woolwich, John Robinson's book *Honest to God*, sank without a trace.

I was fortunate to be aware that the enemy was sowing tares. Confident in the God of the good seed, I was determined to sow, sow and keep sowing. I was from my conversion incredibly privileged to sit under the ministry of the Doctor ... Dr Martyn Lloyd-Jones at Westminster Chapel. If I couldn't get there during my training, then I drank from the Word at Uxbridge Road Tabernacle, when the Rev. John Savage Snr was the Baptist Minister. It was like a breath of spring air to be there, until a storm started to break out!

John had asked me to help him with some church work, exactly what, I cannot quite remember. I promised him I would, requesting the time off. However, at the eleventh hour the Sister refused. Some of the nurses went off sick due to diarrhoea and vomiting, but I was healthy, so I was expected to remain on the ward.

'May I use the telephone to contact a Minister friend of

mine, to let him know I won't be attending his meeting, please?'

'No,' she affirmed. 'Definitely not.'

'But, Sister, the Minister of Uxbridge Road Tabernacle is expecting me.'

She told me she couldn't care less.

When I contacted John the next day to apologise, he didn't let me get a word in edgewise, telling me how I was unreliable, how I'd let him down.

'If you're unreliable here, what'll you do if you eventually go abroad as a missionary?'

'But —.'

He turned his back on me and walked away.

Eventually I did explain, I believe some days afterwards. He and his wife almost became like parents to me. It was he who also baptised Oakley. What a joy! What a delight to see her witness to her faith in such a way.

I met him again when he became the Warden at Datchet. While there I discovered he enjoyed art and was quite nifty with a pencil. I purchased for him some art materials, which gave that lovely saint much joy in the autumn of his years.

Just before the exams, I, laden with textbooks, booked into the Common Cold Centre, then not far from Salisbury Plain. When I wasn't succumbing to daily nasal sprays, throat swabs, and being a general guinea pig in the interests of global science, I had my running nose in a medical textbook, frantically cramming in three years' work.

During my two weeks at the Common Cold Centre, I not only acquired some money, but the mother and father of a cold! On my return to the hospital, I was again admitted to the sick bay. I sat up in my hospital bed swotting for my examinations.

All too soon, the day of the examinations dawned. Yes, I could answer the first question, and the second, along with everything else required of me. I was sure I'd done well, but I

joined my colleagues in saying how awful every question was, and what I would do when I failed — a sort of false modesty.

The results of the Hospital exams were eventually pinned on to the notice board in the School of Nursing. I had passed! I had also passed with excellent marks.

Shortly afterwards, the results of my State finals were delivered by the postman. Gingerly I tore open the large brown envelope. Yes, I was now a qualified Nurse. A Registered General Nurse at last.

'Well, now, good ol' St Jude, eh?' chuckled Miss Prince.

'Who on earth is St Jude?' I asked, turning to face the tutor.

'Oh, he's the saint for hopeless cases,' she explained. 'I prayed to him for you. So thanks to St Jude, eh?'

The tutor even placed 'Thanks to St Jude' in the personal column of the Daily Telegraph newspaper!

7

Called to Serve?

*'Do you not say, "Four months more and then the harvest"?
I tell you, open your eyes and look at the fields!
They are ripe for harvest.'*

(John 4:35)

I was just over halfway through my obstetric experience and the day had been quite a happy one. Under supervision I had delivered a woman of a healthy son. She and her husband were truly delighted.

However, now it was a little after half past five; I was off duty with other concerns. Quite unexpectedly, I'd received a phone call from a friend, asking me to take her Sunday school class; she wasn't feeling too well.

'I've got a stinker of a cold,' she explained. 'I just won't be up to taking it.'

'Honestly, Linda, I'm really not the person to ask. I virtually know nothing about Sunday school work,' I protested. 'In fact, I've never even attended a Christian Sunday school.'

She assured me it would be no irksome duty; on that particular Sunday at South Wimbledon Methodist Church, I

wouldn't have to do very much more than simply supervise the children, so there wouldn't even be any preparation.

'Someone from the Methodist Missionary Society will be visiting to talk about his work. I'm pretty certain he'll be showing some of his slides. All you have to do is welcome him while keeping the children seated and in some order. See, Sarah, there'll be nothing to it,' she croaked. 'You *will* do it for me, won't you? *Please* say you will. Everyone else seems too busy.'

'So, you mean I'm your last resort?' I chuckled. 'All right. Just as well I have the time off, huh?'

It was nothing like as easy as Linda had made out. After opening in prayer, I had to lead everyone with the singing of a few choruses, whilst attempting to play an out of tune piano before introducing the speaker. I then suddenly had one of those terrible moments when one's mind goes blank — I forgot the speaker's name! However, I think I half got away with it by saying, 'This afternoon, children, we have a missionary with us who's going to tell us all about his work before showing us some of his slides. Now, I'll leave him to introduce himself ...' I stepped back clapping my hands.

All the children joined in the clapping; they cheered and one or two whistled — the sort of whistle achieved by putting two fingers in their mouths. The sound which came out was an embarrassing, piercing sound.

One of the missionary's final slides vividly illustrated a large golden cornfield; the corn was shown gently waving in the breeze with the crop ready for harvesting.

'Perhaps, one day, God might call one of you to be a harvester for Him,' he said, a frown on his brow. 'There will be many souls lost to Jesus if there is no one to tell them about His salvation.'

I don't know if God spoke to any of the children in the meeting, but I realised, for the first time in my life, there was a sphere of service to which I might be called; I needed to be

prepared to go wherever He wanted me.

Before any possible service overseas, however, there was one small journey I felt I should make. For years I had attempted to banish my thoughts about the tombstone. Yet once I had allowed the memories, they'd come back and fill my spare moments. Finally, in an attempt to both quieten my mind and deal with my surging curiosity once and for all, I searched for a slot in my diary and made my way to the south London cemetery.

My feet crunched over the gravel path and I stared down at the overgrown stone. A shudder passed over me, not because of any sorrowful memories, but because of the wintry cold. Unlike the day when Lois gave me the news, I neither feared it nor dreaded it. Without staying more than a minute or two, feeling nothing, I walked away.

Although I wasn't exactly ecstatic about seeing it, I knew my eyes weren't upon an old overgrown gravestone; my eyes were upon that Rock which is higher than I, and they still are!

Some weeks later four of my Christian friends from Westminster Chapel told me they were going to Herne Bay Court for a long weekend conference, run by the Poona and Indian Village Mission which was operating in Western India. They invited me to the conference too.

It was, for me, a most memorable weekend when I learned of that great continent of India and I quickly began to develop a deep compassion for those without Christ.

Was God calling me to be a harvester in India? If so, I needed to keep the goal in view; never allowing myself to put it on hold.

Through the reading of Colossians 1:11 the Lord began to show me my need of patience. Patience! A quality my closest friends rarely saw in me, for I always wanted something performed 'yesterday'.

Many of God's choice servants have had to learn the hard

lessons of patience. For example, David was anointed to be King of Israel, but he had to wait many years until the death of Saul, before it came to pass. During this time of waiting, many trials and tribulations came his way, but out of them all David was able to say, *'I waited patiently for the Lord,'* (Psalm 40:1)

I was so keen to go overseas that, in my naivety, about any place would do, just as long as I was a missionary!

I started attending a prayer meeting for the Red Sea Mission Team. This was held in the Finchley home of Dr and Mrs Gurney, and it was there I occasionally met missionaries on furlough. It occurred to me how God might want me as one of their missionary recruits; but someone, in their wisdom, pointed out to me the danger of a Jewess working in a Muslim culture. No. It wasn't for me.

A month or so later there was the valedictory service, held at Westminster Chapel, for one of its members who was leaving to work overseas with the Grenfell Mission. I quickly abandoned any thoughts of working as a midwife in the frozen wastelands. It was not for me.

Realising I wasn't going to be of use to any missionary society while entertaining so many crazy romantic notions, I decided to spend as much time as I could in praying about my future, both privately and with others — mostly friends of roughly my own age.

The young folk linked with the Poona and Village Mission and based in England had been named 'The Harvesters'. I was one of those Harvesters and we were all planning to meet at the Datchet Evangelical Fellowship in Suffolk.

Raymond Castro, a P.I.V.M. committee member, planned to lead those of us eager to spread the Word of God. Three had recently left Mount Hermon Missionary Training College. Two of the three, Rosemary and Margaret, were preparing to leave these shores to work in the Western Indian State of

Maharashtra, under the umbrella of the P.I.V.M. Another, William, was planning to enter the Baptist ministry, once he'd completed his time at Spurgeon's College. Oakley and I were the youngest and about to complete our midwifery training.

I'd had quite a tough task acquiring the time to go with the group. Miss Green, one of the assistant matrons, was sure I wasn't due for any more leave.

'It wasn't all that long ago you went away with the Nurses' Christian Fellowship. You had a fortnight's leave then, didn't you?'

I shook my head. 'I only went away for a week,' I corrected. 'We all went camping in Dorset and it was months ago.'

'Whatever. You can't have any more leave this side of your finals.'

'Oh, please, Miss Green —.'

'I'll think about it.'

'But,' I protested, 'I really want to go with the group to ...'

At that moment one of the other assistant matrons entered the office. Miss Green looked up at me, instructing me to wait outside her door.

Four or five minutes later, Miss Green called me back into her office. I attempted to seat myself, but she instructed me to remain standing.

'It seems, nurse, you are entitled to six days holiday leave.'

'So may I go to Datchet after all?'

Miss Green made it clear that she didn't actually care where I went. 'Please yourself,' she stated.

Oakley and I shared one of the on-site grotty caravans, which she and I cleaned from top to bottom. Rosemary and Margaret shared the other caravan. Ray Castro and William stayed in the 'Big House' where many retired missionaries

saw out their days. Meal times allowed us to gather together around a big trestle table in a nearby barn.

Unlike Oakley, who was an amazing cook, I was 'the pits'. When it came to my turn to cook breakfast for the team I placed the frying pan over the gas flame.

When the pan was good and hot and oil was almost smoking I dropped in the seven hens' eggs — minus the shells! Immediately the whites bubbled up, hiding every yolk. At that, my moment of panic, Margaret made her entrance, exclaiming: 'What on earth have you done?'

The seven of us breakfasted on cornflakes and toast! No one fancied a bit of egg white.

During the week of village evangelism I was teamed up to be with Jenny for much of the time. One afternoon, just after lunch, Ray Castro drove us to a nearby row of terrace houses, but we'd apparently been beaten to it by the Jehovah's Witnesses.

'If you're the Jehovah's Witnesses again, you can clear off!' exclaimed one householder after another.

Finally, Jenny and I, having spent most of the early afternoon 'on the knocker' reached the very last house. The woman of the house opened her front door and stared at Jenny and me.

'Before you say anything,' I started, 'you need to know we are most definitely *not* Jehovah's Witnesses ... okay?'

The woman's face broke into a broad grin as she chuckled, 'Well, I am, so come on in!'

Jenny, having just completed a couple of years at Mount Hermon Missionary Training College, when Rev. Meg Foot was the Principal, obviously knew heaps more than me concerning the Bible, so she did the talking. How far we got with the Jehovah's Witness, only the Lord knows.

'Cor, you've been a long time,' exclaimed Ray Castro, who'd been waiting for us in his car — a grey mini which he claimed had the devil in its engine — hence, he'd had nothing

but trouble with it.

Saturday night came and we gave the youngsters, mostly young teenagers from the village, a sausage sizzle. I was *not* chosen to cook! Instead, I gave out tracts, mingled and, what I do best, I talked — talked to them, telling them how great it was to be a Christian. I invited them to attend the church at Stratford St Mary. They shrugged. One of them told me he'd never been to a church service. Another explained he only had jeans and a T-shirt, so surely he couldn't attend.

'Fine, we're not interested in what you'll be wearing. We'll just be glad to see you. Isn't that right?' I said to him, at the same time looking for support from the others. However, those were the days when we women wouldn't have dared to turn up in anything but our Sunday best, complete with hats, so they didn't know quite how to answer me.

The next day, the Lord's Day, the seven of us appeared in togs worthy of the Buckingham Palace Garden Party! I hoped upon hope the lads would turn up, but they didn't. Ray Castro was the preacher both morning and evening. Halfway through his morning service a black and white cat jumped up in the pulpit, causing smiles all around, yet not from Ray.

'Would someone be so kind as to remove this moggy, please?' he asked.

Before the week was up we all had a day's break in Lowestoft, piling on the beach to relax. As a joke ... a bit of fun ... Ray buried my sandals in the sand. When it was time to return to Datchet everyone tried to help him to find my footwear, yet without success. Barefooted, I found it quite difficult to pick my way back. William told me to lean on him.

Suddenly a friendship began to blossom and Oakley felt she was playing gooseberry.

Once the week was drawing to a close, William asked if he could carry on seeing me. I agreed. For about a month or

so, we continued our meetings, but then the day came when he was supposed to collect me in his old blue Ford for a date. I waited and waited; so, when it was obvious he wasn't going to arrive, I went back into the Nurses' Home, located his number at Spurgeon's College and asked to speak to him.

'I'm afraid he's not in right now,' came a man's deep voice. 'Sorry. Anyway, may I take a message?'

'Yes. He was supposed to meet me this evening. I waited and waited, but he didn't turn up.'

'Oh, you must be Sally.'

'What?'

'Well, after your wedding ... what is it ... only five or six weeks to go and then ...'

'Excuse me, but what are you talking about? — We're not getting married. Have you got the right fellow?'

'William. We're on about William, eh? And you're Sally.'

'I'm Sarah. Not Sally. I think I've been two-timed.' I replaced the receiver.

I spoke with Ray Castro regarding William.

'He's been a bad lad, hasn't he, stringing you along, and all the time planning his wedding with another. Oh, I feel so sorry for you, Sarah.'

I felt sorry for me too; hurt and angry.

8

Restoration and Renewal

I no longer felt aware of any Divine purpose at work in my life. Although I wouldn't outwardly admit it, I was in fact becoming somewhat depressed, as if God had cast me aside since I'd left behind me all the familiarities of London, my friends and colleagues there. It was, however, in a mood of grim determination that I arrived in the North of England, way north of Watford and what I saw before me as a tortuous path.

The north-bound train in which I found myself began, without any warning, to make an ear splitting noise; the next moment it gave a kind of lurching jump before coming to a full stop. A passenger was heard to yell that we were going to crash. A verbal dispute broke out between a skinny driver and a tall, fat man, both clad in official British Rail uniforms, both either shouting at each other or aggressively waving their arms in the air. Their words flowing past me in an incomprehensible daze, I left the carriage, jumped down onto the platform and promptly approached a porter who appeared ready to join in the terms of abuse, he taking the side of the driver.

'Excuse me,' I interrupted, pulling my thick winter coat around me, my breath, as I spoke, showing a long frosty

stream. 'I need to get to Rotherham. Did you hear? I need to get to Rotherham in South Yorkshire.'

'Ooh aye.'

'Well, am I far from there? Will it take long to get there?'

He shrugged his shoulders. 'Could do. Depends about this 'ere driver.'

'If it's going to take a long time, could I get a taxi from here, please?'

'Depends. Depends, if you'd like to walk ... or you'd like to ride.'

'On what? What does it depend upon?'

'On 'ow fit th'art. Th'sees, th'art in Doncaster reet nah!'

'What? What did you say? I didn't quite understand.'

A frigid wind created havoc with the dark shapes of the trees, and the scant light of the moon made everywhere seem to me foreign and foreboding as I made my way to Rotherham's Wilcox Green, where I'd been told I could have an apartment on the second floor.

There were plenty of street lights and the routes were well marked. I asked the cab driver to stop at the village store, but it was closed.

'I'm not going to have anything to drink — not a cup of tea or coffee — and I hate it without milk,' I told him.

'Look, why don't you come home with me? It's over the other side of town. It's really not that far. My wife 'll soon sort things out for you. I'll drop you off on the way so you can make sure your place is properly locked up.'

I worried. Lesser mortals had died at the hands of such strangers and I was becoming terrified by what this man might do to me. Fearing the pain I might suffer before the death, fearing for my own life, adrenaline rushed through my blood like lightning and I stared at him. He read my reaction.

'You'll be safe. This isn't the East End of London you know!' he said. 'It's a maze back to your apartment, so I'll

drive you back later.'

Wordlessly, I remained in his car, watching his strong, hairy hands on the wheel, and my heart pounded nineteen to the dozen.

'Will you like work here? What did you say you're gonna do?'

'I didn't.'

'What then?'

'I'm going to become a Health Visitor. I'll be working under the watchful eye of a fieldwork instructor. I met her when I was interviewed.'

'Who's that then?'

'Mrs Spearing.'

He smiled. 'Yeah. I know her. She was a real brick when the wife had our little lad. What we didn't know, well, she put us straight.'

'Good.'

He drove on to the smart Hallam Road, pulling into the drive of a house halfway down. The house was all in darkness.

'Strange,' he said, his brow knitting together. 'I wonder where the wife is.'

'And your child, too, huh?' I questioned, believing I had been tricked.

However, just as I was about to give him a piece of my mind a neighbour, a petite woman in her late fifties appeared from the next detached house.

'Hallo, my dear,' she said, sympathy showing across her kind face. 'Anna's in here with me. She brought in little Jack and he's fallen asleep on our settee, bless him. Are you going to come in? And who is this?'

'Oh, hallo. I'm Sarah ... Sarah Cohen.'

'I'm Peggy ... Peggy Hardcastle. Ooh, it's freezing cold out here. Come on in and get warm and then you can tell me all about yourself.'

During the following week I found the local butcher. I had only been in my new job for a few days when I met Peggy and her husband, Sidney, for the second time. To repay their hospitality I had invited them to my 'new' home for an evening meal — seven o'clock, to eat at seven-thirty.

'What do you recommend?' I asked the butcher. 'I wondered about your very best beef ...'

He positioned himself on the other side of the counter and I felt his scrutiny as if he was dissecting me as thoroughly as a side of beef.

'So you must be related to Mrs Hardcastle?' He posed the comment as if a challenge.

'Oh, no. Not at all. Why did you assume ...?'

He grinned. 'It's just that you speak as posh as she does!'

I chuckled. 'You obviously know her well.'

He told me she'd been a good customer of his for almost ten years. 'So you've come to live around here?'

'I'm Miss Cohen,' I replied. 'I'm joining the Health Visiting team. Anyway, about this meat ...'

Finally, I paid the butcher what I owed him and we made our goodbyes. I was delighted with my purchase, especially as he'd even recommended the cooking instructions — because I knew I wasn't the finest of cooks.

'It's so good of you to come.' I motioned to Sidney and Peggy to enter. 'Please do come in.'

My hallway was long and thin, leading through to a formal lounge-cum-dining room and into the kitchen. Furniture was spanking new, and elegant. A Chinese rug was almost the size of the living area, and I'd framed three of my own paintings left over from my time in Wimbledon College of Art and Design. The kitchen was functional, yet it gave the impression I wasn't at home.

Peggy did most of the talking, telling me with pride about their two sons. 'They really are the lights of our lives.'

'But of course we have the old girl who keeps us fit!'

Sidney added with a grin.

'That's our Mutty.'

'He means our little cairn terrier,' she laughed. 'And what about you, my dear?'

After a fresh fruit salad, I made coffees, but Peggy asked for just tea so weak it was virtually milk and water! She began to ask one question after another, devastated when I told her about my rotten experience with William. I'd planned to say nothing, but she had a way of picking up on all the details, wheedling out about my love life — or rather lack of it.

'Are you a bit like Jonah? He tried to go where he shouldn't have and that certainly rocked the boat, didn't it?' Peggy questioned in a blunt direct way, which didn't hurt my feelings. 'Anyway, perhaps you'd like to come over to Sheffield with us Sunday next?'

'Sheffield?'

Peggy nodded, 'We're going over to Ray Beeley's church for the evening service,' she pushed.

My voice trembled. 'Well, um, oh, yes. All right. Why not?'

If I had refused she'd have probably wanted to know why, so it was best to say yes.

'Come for Sunday lunch first. Oh, please do.'

I began to attend Broom Methodist Church in Rotherham, which was then Peggy's spiritual home.

At first I didn't really intend going anywhere too often. However, it was easier to agree to go to the Sunday services than to make my apologies to this spiritual giant.

Peggy also longed to see me 'courting' with a view to marriage. She tried to see me fixed up with this one and that, but when her matchmaking came to naught she worried.

'Oh, you don't want to be left on the shelf, do you?' Peggy protested, a concerned look across her face. 'Will you be happy as an old maid?'

I told her I would be! When I did meet a man however, she was truly delighted.

Peggy could never remember his name and, as he'd originated from Huddersfield, she usually questioned me as to how things were progressing with my "Mr Huddersfield".

I had the privilege of knowing Peggy Hardcastle for a total of thirty-five precious years, until, in her ninety-third year, she was called home to be with the Saviour she adored.

To me, to my "Mr Huddersfield" and to our three lovely sons, she was so special. To our three boys she was known as "Nanna Castle".

She had nicknamed me her 'adopted daughter', rarely saying my Christian name, naming me either 'my dear' or 'darling'. I miss her desperately.

During my time in Rotherham a Mr Harper, who then ran quite a large Christian bookshop in the town, introduced himself to me, stating how he'd heard all about me from Peggy Hardcastle.

'Peggy knows my wife and me quite well,' he said. 'In fact, we were only at the Hardcastles' last week for Sunday lunch. She was telling us all about you.'

I wasn't surprised.

Mr Harper explained how she'd told him about my background. 'I believe you come from a Jewish family,' he said. 'God's chosen race, eh?'

'Well, yes, but that's all in the past. I'm a Christian now, so —'

'So you're a believer. Right. However, you don't stop being Jewish, do you?'

'I don't? I thought I did.'

'No, you definitely do not.'

I wondered what he was getting at. Anyway, moments later Mr Harper was roping me in to not only giving my testimony, but he was flicking through his diary to arrange a time when I could give a Passover demonstration.

'It'll help the congregation to understand why they take communion,' he added.

'I'll need to have help.'

'Whatever. About how many? And what do you need?'

Two weeks later, on the Thursday just before Easter, I began giving a word of testimony, explaining how I came into a saving knowledge of the Lord Jesus Christ, and then how the Orthodox part of my family erected a headstone in the Jewish cemetery following my baptism in water. After a few gasps of horror from some of the older congregation, I then began, with help from Mr Harper himself, along with a willing nine-year-old who played his part beautifully.

We had the Seder plate 1 with a shank bone from the Rotherham butcher, the haroseth, the bitter herbs, and the roasted egg. Candles were lit, non-alcoholic wine was consumed and we sang and clapped a lot. There was the ritual handwashing, but when I broke the matzos in half, I had to hide the other half, known as the aphikomen; one elderly man, slightly hard of hearing, thought it was something to do with a chap called "Alfy Cohen," which made more than a few chuckle at the error.

When the youngster searched for the aphikomen everyone shouted: 'hotter' or 'colder' depending on how near the boy was to it. When he discovered it, I gave him a gift. As he unwrapped an illustrated book about 'Daniel in the Lions' Den' many craned their necks to see what it was.

I enjoyed being with the Harpers, fellowshipping with them at their church, their bookshop, their home and my apartment. Above all, they restored in me the confidence to speak in public, to work for the Lord. When I knew they'd been promoted to Glory, I also missed them greatly.

9

Are Two Better Than One?

It was 'Last of the Summer Wine' country, the home of the actress, Nora Batty, with her wrinkled stockings, so I had been told. From the very moment when I first arrived in Holmfirth, the beauty of the surrounding countryside entranced me. Whatever the mood of the weather, a day rarely passed without catching my breath in surprise and delight at one thing or another. In an infinite number of small and grand ways, nature in all its glory was constantly revealing itself to me in this corner of West Yorkshire.

Turning left, I strolled along to the little Methodist chapel, enjoying the walk, after being cooped up in the office some of the day, where I was employed as a Health Visitor's assistant.

There he was again. I had seen him before, and a faint smile touched my mouth. The man did not have glamorous movie star looks, although he was reasonably good looking in a clean-cut way. His slightly receding hair was dark, his eyes a chocolate brown, their expression gentle, and his mouth was quick to smile.

He was about five foot nine in height. A pleasant, ordinary sort of guy I decided, as he seated himself in the pew

where I was sitting. Spellbound, as I seemed to be, he was older than me, maybe old enough to be too old. I wasn't sure.

After the evening service, I went across to shake hands with this enigmatic stranger, but he'd turned to speak to someone else. I was left standing, and I felt a bit of a chump!

With God central again in my life, I knew He had plans for me: *'For I know the plans I have for you, for welfare and not for evil, to give you a future and a hope.'* (Jeremiah 29:11). As for my future, I didn't yet know who or what it involved. All I needed to do was trust my loving heavenly Father each step of the way, taking each day as it came.

Aware I was new to the area, and having seen me in church, the also new Methodist Superintendent Minister visited my house to see me; a sort of pastoral visit to introduce himself.

'Oh, um, by the way, I wonder if you know the man who was sitting by me last Sunday?' I asked, promptly describing this stranger in much detail.

'Oh, I think that must be Eric. He's the one who likes photography.'

Photography, eh? Hmm, my mind was knitting away nineteen to the dozen.

The Minister nodded. 'Why, do you like photography, too?' he questioned.

'What?' I grinned, a twinkle in my eyes. 'Oh, not yet.'

That week I purchased a new Olympus SLR camera, not even knowing how to put it together, once I had it out of its box. The following Sunday I eventually managed to come face to face with Eric. 'I've been hearing how you're a keen photographer ...' I began.

'Yes, I like photography very much indeed. Why do you ask?'

I informed him how I'd acquired a new camera, but I didn't quite know how to work it, and maybe he could show me.

He agreed. 'I've a day off this Thursday, and I'm planning to go to Sheffield to photograph the cathedral. Perhaps you'd like to come along? It'd give you a chance to get the hang of your new camera.'

Various outings followed, and we decided to continue our friendship, until one evening, just before we were about to go to our respective homes, he stared at me, with a peculiar expression on his face ... a sort of silly grin.

'What's wrong?' I asked.

'I love you, Sarah, I really am in love with you.'

I gaped at him. 'What? What did you say?'

'You heard what I said.' Eric, there and then, went down on one knee. 'Will you marry me? Please, Sarah, say you will.'

We celebrated our engagement at the Three Nuns, a restaurant in Yorkshire's Mirfield. The soft candlelight threw a warm and rosy glow over the scene, which seemed to be a reflection of our feelings — our romance, a romance for life, till death us do part.

From the moment we announced our engagement, life became a matter of decisions; an exciting whirl of plans and preparations. My dress, my shoes, a bridesmaid, the cake, and the flowers. There was then our first home to organise; colours, fabrics, plates and glasses, table linen, pretty sheets for the bedrooms and carpets for the floor. What to choose? Where to start? There was so much to do, until he eventually became *my* "Mr Huddersfield"!

Paul, the first born, delighted us, having entered our world on the twentieth of August 1971. He was just beautiful, although he soon acquired severe eczema down the sides of his lovely face, on his hands and in his joints. Peggy Hardcastle, who adored babies to bits, made him cool, cotton vests and shirts to try to relieve his itch; they helped him no end, as did various creams and prescribed potions — for a while.

Paul gave us so much pleasure that it seemed obvious another little brother or sister would enhance our family.

On 28th November 1973 I went into labour. The winter snow lay thick on the ground and my "Mr Huddersfield" started to clear the drive so he could get me into the Huddersfield Royal Infirmary's labour ward.

We'd arranged for a local neighbour to care for Paul during our absence, but our then two-year-old, never having been left by me previously, didn't like the idea. He stood in the doorway, clutching a neighbour's hand.

'Oh, Mummy, Mummy, don't leave me, don't leave me,' he sobbed. 'Mummy stay with me here.'

'I'm coming back, you know,' I called to him, but Paul wasn't listening.

When, a couple of days later, I returned home again, cuddling a beautiful, fair-haired baby boy who I'd named Stephen, Paul looked even more upset.

'What's the matter, Paul?' I asked, giving him a kiss.

'I don't want him,' he told me. 'Stamp him out. Take him back. Stamp him out!'

'But,' I protested, 'he's your little baby brother. His name is Stephen. Isn't he just gorgeous?'

Paul shook his head. 'I'll call him "Stampy out". I want to stamp him out, so I'll name him "Stampy out".'

I have since discovered such jealousy can be considerably reduced if the first child's initial sight of the new baby isn't in the parent's arms.

However, the apparent upset and jealousy didn't last and, as they grew, they became best of friends — usually! They had their moments.

When Paul was thirteen and Stephen eleven, I started to feel sick, craving cold porridge, salad cream sandwiches and pineapple juice. Tea and coffee made me feel I wanted to throw up. It didn't take a genius to work out that I was pregnant again.

During the end of my third pregnancy the consultant obstetrician told me, having palpated my abdomen, something quite unexpected.

'You'll need an elective Caesarean Section. The baby is a breech and, to try and deliver it vaginally, well, we could place the baby at risk.'

That evening we went to a prayer meeting at the Methodist church where we were members. This minister and his wife, Anne, were parents of two-year-old twins, and we were able to share things with them. After the meeting we stayed behind for a coffee, and I told them that I was to have a Caesarean Section because the baby was in a breech position.

'Would you like Anne and me to pray for you?' the minister asked me in his quiet voice.

I was surprised by the suggestion. After the obstetrician's authoritative pronouncement, it didn't occur to me that it was a matter of prayer, for it all seemed so final.

'If you want to,' I replied with a sigh. 'Why not?'

They prayed and, as they did, the baby seemed more active than ever. This also seemed to increase my heartburn and breathlessness from which I suffered during the latter part of the pregnancy.

The following week, I, still with my 'bump', waddled along to yet another antenatal check-up. I breathlessly climbed onto a couch, and awaited the arrival of the obstetrician.

She marched into the cubicle and began to feel how the baby was lying.

'That's funny,' she said, 'most odd.'

'What is?' I asked, feeling a little worried.

She ignored my questions and called for the Senior Midwife. Complete panic seemed to fill my whole being. Whatever was wrong? Why was she calling for the midwife? Why would she not answer my question when I asked what was wrong?

The midwife came and palpated my abdomen. She agreed it was funny ... funny peculiar.

'What's wrong?' I asked in a louder tone. 'Tell me, please!'

'Nothing, absolutely nothing!' came the obstetrician's answer with a smile. She told me that the baby had turned, although it was actually too big to do so.

It was now coming head first, instead of buttocks or feet first, and so I would not be needing a Caesarean Section. I would have a normal delivery after all unless, of course, anything else went wrong in labour.

'I don't understand how that could have happened though,' said the obstetrician, frowning and shaking her head. 'Most odd.'

I explained that the minister and his wife prayed for me about the position of the baby.

On the following Friday morning at 6 A.M. I began to have severe backache. The contractions started. I told my husband it was time to go to the hospital. He raced to get the car out of the garage. My small suitcase was thrown onto the back seat. He then stopped in his tracks and realised that it would be a good idea if he put me into the car too!

The hospital was quite a long drive from where we lived, and we seemed to catch every red traffic light along the way.

On arrival at the Bradford Hospital, I was taken to a private room, where I was examined. The contractions were coming thick and fast, but they were not causing the labour to progress. At 3 P.M. I was given medication to rectify things. It worked!

The midwife was suddenly assisting the delivery of our baby, whilst my husband was still trying to tie up the back of her sterile green gown. At 3:25 P.M. a baby cried. We had another son! It was a normal delivery. It was a happy day — one to treasure forever, even though it seemed long and arduous for me. The midwife began to tell Eric to give me a

kiss. She was too late. I was holding our new son in one arm, and the other arm was round my husband's neck as he kissed me. He was so overcome by the whole emotional experience that I could feel his wet, salty tears on my face.

We were now a complete family.

Matthew was perfect, weighing in at 8lb 2oz, on 31st August 1984. All three of our children, although brought up in the same way, with the same values, are so different.

Paul was the quietest. However, on one occasion, he had plenty to say!

In 1979 we owned quite a large house which was within walking distance of the chapel where we were members. However, one Sunday some missionaries on furlough needed somewhere to have lunch. The Pastor asked if we would be their hosts. We agreed.

Paul had previously asked me if we could have new colour TV. In those days most folk still owned black and white TVs. I told Paul we couldn't afford one. Over the dessert one of the missionaries looked around and asked if we owned one of the new colour TVs. I shook my head, explaining how we couldn't afford one.

Suddenly, Paul piped up: 'We would be able to have a new colour TV if we didn't have to keep feeding missionaries, such as you!' There were reddened faces all round, mine especially!

Continuing with memories of laughter, Stephen was probably about seven when he finally mastered his two-wheeled bike, abandoning the stabilisers. Delighted with himself, he cycled down a nearby hill, much too fast, and went over the handlebars, fracturing his right arm — which meant a brief absence from school.

As a treat and an attempt to cheer him up, I drove Stephrn into the nearby town to have a lunch out. Well, that was the plan!

'Hey, look, Stephen, there's a nice-looking café, and it doesn't seem to have any customers yet. We'll virtually have the place to ourselves,' I told him.

We chose a really lovely table, a window seat.

'There's no menu, Mummy,' Stephen said.

'Oh, I'm sure the waiter will bring us one. Here he comes now.'

'Good day, madam,' said a very smartly-dressed young man. 'How may I help you?'

'Well, we're not quite sure.'

'This table's very nice ...' he began.

'Yes, it is nice to have one in the window.'

Now the fellow was looking quite confused, but anyway I asked for Stephen to have a strawberry milkshake, and I'd have a coffee — a dash of milk with no sugar.

'Pardon, madam?'

I repeated the order.

'Madam, this isn't a café. You're sitting in the window of our furniture showroom! The table and chairs are for sale!'

The youngest of our three sons, Matthew, who was born in 1984, was no less able to provide a memorable moment. When he was five he was enrolled into an excellent prep school, and my part-time work as a Registered Nurse helped to pay the fees.

One day, shopping in a nearby town, I happened to meet one of the teachers from the school. During our conversation she told me how Matthew informed a colleague of hers that I'd said I could do better than her academically and could do so standing on my head!

What have I learned? Don't say things in front of your children if you don't want to be embarrassed — or found out!

10

Paul's Final Journey

In 1985 my husband arranged for us as a family to holiday for two weeks in a static caravan, not very far from Church Fenton's airfield. Paul, on his thirteenth birthday, had been treated to a pleasure flight from Southport to Blackpool. From then on he was bitten by the flying bug. Now, here we were a year later; he could hardly wait to be taken to see RAF Church Fenton, just to view the planes.

Eleven years later I received the following letter through the post:

Atlanta, Georgia,
U.S.A.
1996

Dear Mum,
It's the morning of my third day since arriving in Atlanta, my holiday base for the following seven weeks. I have just spread a large topographical map across the kitchen table, searching for a place my destiny would take me. I'm so excited.

Facing the window of bright sunlight, I can just

77

focus on my Cessna aircraft; yesterday it appeared as a mirage, shimmering through this sweltering heat rising from the melting tarmac. Mopping the perspiration from my brow with the back of my forearm, the location of this airfield, so I've been told, will present me with a wide range of flight possibilities, being sixty miles south of Chattanooga, ninety miles east of Athens (nowhere near Greece!), and Birmingham, Alabama, is only one hundred and twenty miles to the west.

Pinpointing a small, out of the way airfield by the name of Cullowhee, approximately a mere eighty miles north-east of Rome, Georgia, I joked with Chad how the place sounded more like a Red Indian brave!

Chad, a pilot much more experienced than I, especially within the field of navigation, is a tall, white man born and bred in the South. Normally a happy-go-lucky, a bright and breezy guy, he told me: 'Paul, see that place as off limits.' He began, looking unusually stern, 'Cullowhee is an extremely dangerous and difficult place to find from the air. Even if you do locate it, you'll most likely have difficulties landing . . . and with only a slim chance of survival.'

'Why's that?' I asked.

'The length of the runway . . . it's insufficient. You'd be a dummy to take such a gigantic gamble.'

Never one to either turn away a challenge or be accused of lacking in moral fibre, I shrugged at Chad, firm in my resolve to go to Cullowhee, even though the odds seemed heavily weighted against me.

Next day: having gone through the pre-flight

checks and filled the aircraft with twenty gallons of fuel (comparatively cheap stuff here in America), I am ready for the off. When I taxi out to the runway, I will consider myself fortunate to be flying on such a beautiful morning. The sky above is an azure blue, the perfect backcloth for the cumulus clouds now forming in streets, just as if they might lead me straight on to my destination where I'd reach a part, it's true to say, few airlines do not reach! But I'll have a go at it.

Having made the obligatory call: 'Rome traffic, Cessna November five six niner golf', I'm positioned and holding for departure runway one at Rome, and having positioned my aircraft on the centre line of the runway, I gently eased in the throttle and the plane began to vibrate. Releasing the brakes, the machine thrust forward with an eager anticipation.

Reaching sixty miles an hour, I was airborne and on my way to a hazardous destination, barely seen on my map.

Drawing close to my intended altitude of three thousand feet, I gently eased back the throttle until the 'revs per minute gauge' read 2,100. Adjusting the mixture for economy cruising and correcting the directional giro to the exact heading by using the standard compass, I checked the time between waypoints and my estimated time of arrival (E.T.A.). So far, everything was spot on.

Settling into my routine, I began to fly more via sole reference to ground objects. This proved much more fun, giving me the opportunity to take in the golden expanse of geometric patterned wheat fields reaching to touch the foothills of the Appalachian Mountains over to my right.

Dripping with sweat, I was hotter still in the cockpit, as the sun beat down.

The intended eighty miles had passed and, according to the navigational system, along with my mathematical calculations, the aircraft, dead on course, was right above Cullowhee, a small town situated on the bank of a meander in the River Tennessee.

After almost fifteen precious minutes of circling, searching, I could just see the barely visible makeshift runway some three thousand feet below. The map gave the length of the runway as eighteen hundred feet; yet it now seemed unusable with a large mound of gravel piled high at one end.

'Ah well!' I exclaimed. 'I've jolly well come this far – so here goes . . .'

Easing back the throttle and making the mixture rich again, I began to spirally descend over the airfield.

Carburettor heat was on and the altimeter was winding down hurriedly due to the high sink rate. Entering a down wind leg parallel to the runway at fifteen hundred feet, Cullowhee came into full view. If I knew no better, I could easily have been landing at the film set from "The Little House On The Prairie"! Much concentration, almost terrifying in its intensity, was needed at this point to avoid the umpteen telegraph wires criss-crossing the runway on final approach – not to mention the grain silo!

The wind suddenly became incredibly strong and I fought the rudders of lateral control onto final approach. Easing in the final stage of flap, fighting desperately hard with the prevailing headwind and ground turbulence, the wheels touched down

heavily and the Cessna slewed in every direction but straight on the loose gravel.

Mercifully, the aircraft came to a standstill with a sickening jolt . . . and with only fifty feet of runway left. Parking the craft, I was now concerned as to whether the length of the runway would allow me a long enough take-off to get out of the place. Secretly, I was frightened and alone; yet, with a mixture of anxiety and pride in what I'd accomplished, I shall return to Chad, convincing him that it will not be quite as difficult to do again.

Love to you all,

Paul x

Soon to be our good-humoured, unmarried son Paul's twenty-seventh birthday, he decided to celebrate his occasion with another trip to America. He planned to hire a Piper single-engined aircraft from a company in Daytona Beach, Florida, and explore the Bahamas, a little off Haiti and Jamaica before meeting up with a long-standing friend, Emma, now a commercial pilot, in the Cayman Islands.

When Paul told me of his plans I almost wished he'd kept a veil of secrecy over them. Looking into his large brown eyes, I nervously expressed my parental concern: 'A single-engined plane ... what if that one engine fails? And Haiti of all places ... Oh, Paul!'

'Mum you're a born worrier,' he chuckled, smoothing back his short, curly, light brown hair. 'I'm no longer a little kid. Nothing'll happen to me. Anyway, flying's character building!'

However, on 29th August 1998, I felt weak in the knees; my worst fears were realised as I received distressing news from Stephen, then news from the Foreign Office, how the Piper plane (Registration N25626) was missing.

During World War II the Air Ministry's almost daily

communiqués, via the BBC's announcers, were that 'some of our aircraft are missing'. There was something impersonal in that, for it was about machines rather than men. There was a feeling of history as my husband and I were informed about the missing Piper.

All we knew was that Paul radioed his intentions to Haiti's air traffic control; then suddenly, the little green blip which was his plane, disappeared from the radar screen.

Somewhere out there, abruptly and for reasons unknown, the Piper came down in the Caribbean Sea.

When his disappearance became known the US coastguard mounted a search for him, yet without success. Alas, Paul's life left an inconclusive ending.

Over the Caribbean Sea, maybe somewhere between Cuba and Haiti, on his way to see Emma and to celebrate his 27th birthday, his time ran out. All of Paul's resilience and skill were obviously of no avail over an expanse of sea which has secretly claimed many victims; the Piper plane disappeared without a trace.

What I suppose I'd fastened on, after a great deal of philosophising, was my hope he'd return some day and I would hear his cheery voice, feel the firm grip on my shoulder, kissing my cheek, telling me not to worry, I would watch his dark eyes and listen to him speak to me, and it'd seem as though he had never been away.

However, it won't happen. No one on this earth shall ever see, touch or hear Paul again. Although it is a terrible loss of a young life, yet I am comforted by the knowledge that he died doing what he loved — flying. I am also comforted knowing how he'll be in the presence of the Lord he had come to know, and I'll definitely see him again in heaven. Yet I miss him now, every day more than I feel I can tolerate. Christmases, birthdays, Mothering Sundays — he's just not there and I ache.

11

To Russia with Love

'**W**hat shall I wear for this evening?' I asked Eric on the Friday. Only I would want to know. Other people might not care, but I was to be on show, as it were.

'Something which won't distract anyone from your talk,' he suggested. It was a pretty vain hope and, dare I say, a slightly foolish suggestion, for I didn't consider that my wardrobe included any clothes which did distract. Like so many other ladies, I often complained to my husband I had nothing to wear!

'But what, exactly?' I queried.

'I like you in blue,' he said. 'Wear something in that colour.'

I wasn't being easy to please. I said, 'I could wear my blue skirt with a white blouse.'

'You will look marvellous. Now, come on.'

'You'd tell me honestly, wouldn't you? I don't look awful, do I?'

Eric assured me he would tell me the truth, and reminded me of the time. I hate being late; in fact, I'm often much too early — embarrassingly early!

It was hard to recognise the dusty rugby hall when we

arrived. The place was transformed. Huge posters of Israel festooned two of the walls. There was a table covered in white cloth, holding matzos (unleavened bread) wrapped in cling film, and a silver chalice ready for the wine. There were pink silk flowers too, all beautifully arranged in a dry vase.

We were welcomed as we arrived by Moshe, who was tuning up a guitar. Another man, wearing an Oxford-blue skull cap, had gentle features; he was clapping to the beat.

On seeing us, the guitarist came over to greet Eric and me. 'Now,' he said, 'you must be ...?'

'Sarah,' I replied, offering my hand.

He immediately placed his right hand behind his back, declining to shake my hand. 'And you are a married woman!' he exclaimed. 'Fancy you, of all people, trying to shake my hand!'

Having lived so long outside Jewish circles, I had simply forgotten this particular custom. Attempting to justify myself, I reminded him that, although I had been brought up in the Orthodox way of life, I was now a Christian, under the new covenant.

'A believer!' he quickly corrected. 'We Jews don't use the word Christian in this Messianic congregation.'

Knowing perfectly well that many in Messianic congregations are only partly Jewish or Gentiles with an interest in things Jewish, I peered at his features. 'But you're not Jewish, are you? You don't look Jewish.'

He flushed. 'Well, um, well, whatever, maybe I should introduce you as someone other than Sarah Lockwood. It's so ... Gentile sounding.'

'Sarah is my name, and Sarah Lockwood is my married name,' I replied. 'Cohen was only my maiden name ...'

'Right, I'll introduce you as Sarah Cohen. Sounds much better than Sarah Lockwood. No one will believe you are an Orthodox Jewess with your married name.'

After we'd sung some songs to which everyone clapped a

lot, I, Sarah Cohen, gave my testimony, fully aware that two hostile rabbis were sitting behind me, hanging on to my every word.

'It was truly great to hear how Hashem (God) broke into your life,' said a chap named David.

'You come here regularly?' Eric asked him.

'Oh yes. Every Friday evening when we celebrate the start of the Shabbat.'

'Right. So where, David, do you worship?'

'What do you mean?'

'I mean which church do you attend?'

'Oh no. I am part of this Messianic congregation,' he said. 'I do not attend a Christian church. Neither was I baptised, as you were, Sarah. We are mikvahed. Our sons, by the way, are circumcised, and my eleven-year-old lad is going to be Bar Mitzvahed. Churches just do not understand us Jews. However you fitted into a church, I just do not know!'

'But,' I began to remonstrate, 'I thought the Messianic congregations were supposed to act as a bridge for Jews who'd come to know the Lord Jesus?'

'Yeshua ... Yeshua, not Jesus,' he corrected me again.

'As I was saying,' I started again. 'I understood such places as these were formed to be a bridge from Judaism to Christianity. I do know folk who attend other Messianic congregations, and they do not have a conflict with attending church. Here, it seems, you're going back into the law with your prayer shawls and yarmulkes, and so on.'

Whilst I admired them for the risks they were taking in starting an evangelistic work within a Jewish area of town, I was deeply disturbed by the emphasis they were embracing. I knew, quite clearly, all the apostles were Jewish, and while they frequently attended the synagogue and the temple, their important meeting together was on the first day of the week, a day so special because of the resurrection from the dead of Jesus, the one and only Messiah. Not to lead new believers

into an appreciation of worship on a Sunday, I considered was a mistake.

I wasn't invited again! However, before I did leave, I was provided with some information regarding the refuseniks.

'Refusenik' became an international word to describe a Soviet Jew, who having being consistently refused permission to emigrate to Israel, was harassed by the then KGB (Soviet secret police), usually dismissed from his or her place of work, and lived in fear of arrest on trumped-up charges, which could result in imprisonment.

After praying about the refuseniks, it was as if the Lord was telling me to get up and do something. Three days later, I contacted the Women's Campaign for Soviet Jewry and Rita, a co-chairman, sent me a brief biography of George Belitzskie, along with guidance for letter writing and literature concerning anti-Semitic propaganda in the former USSR.

Anti-Semitism was no novelty, for even during the time of the Czars, many Russian Jews were made to suffer. Stalin arrested and murdered umpteen Jewish leaders. Now anti-Semitism was at the height of Russian fashion.

The list of refuseniks seemed endless, and I knew I couldn't help them all; but I considered I could do something about George Belitzskie, the longest serving refusenik — ten years in all.

A scientist, living in Vilnius, the capital of Lithuania, George and his family first applied to emigrate to Israel in 1980, and were refused then and subsequently, until early 1987 when Margaret, his wife, and Vladimir and Constantine, his two sons, were given permission to emigrate to Israel. As sons were liable to be conscripted into the Soviet Army, the family decided that Margaret and the boys would leave. George was refused permission on the grounds of 'secrecy.' He had worked in the Institute of Mechanics until 1979,

developing a measuring device, which later became the subject of his doctoral thesis. When developing this device, he tested it in a military installation, which to enter, he had to have security clearance. George was not allowed to leave the country for five years after turning in his security pass. His refusal was then extended to 2010. He was made to work as a bookbinder. The family in Israel were adamant that George was not party to any 'secrets', and that he should be given permission to emigrate.

At the end of 1987 Vladimir wrote, in appeal for his father, 'It is impossible to find out which authority was responsible for the "secrecy" in his [George's] case.'

The KGB in Lithuania claimed that the Moscow authorities were responsible for his case, and the Central authorities claimed that the authorities in Lithuania were responsible now that he lived there! George received the impression that nobody was prepared to help him emigrate to Israel.

In the meantime, George became intensely conscious of the many hundreds of Russian Jews who were butchered in World War II. For every seventy thousand Jews brutally killed, George made seventy Stars of David — one for each thousand Jews killed — and placed them before the government's official. He organised a twenty-four-hour vigil, and lit candles in the former ghetto of Vilnius, indicating that George was no meek and mild little man!

George was desperately lonely for his family, and he valued support from the west. Knowing this, I either wrote letters or sent postcards every Wednesday, the day I always wrote to my once estranged Jewish family.

In March 1989 George decided to step up his campaign, and held a demonstration in front of the Ministry of High

Education in Moscow. The Minister promised to review his case. In June, George had his 'secrecy' rating lifted, but he was promptly sent papers for army duty for one month. This would, of course, include more secrecy rating, and make his emigration to Israel impossible.

On 30th August 1989 I received two letters from George. The first said:

George Belitzskie,
Zerucio St 6-55,
Vilnius, 232043
USSR

Dear Sarah,
    Thank you very much for your warm letters. I'm still a refusenik and need your help and support.

Sincerely yours,
Belitzskie

The second letter told me he could not leave to go to Israel, and begged me to help him in his struggle. So it was I stepped up my campaign. I began to either write or to phone every Russian embassy that I could find on the face of the Western earth; everywhere from Canada to Luxembourg, Germany to Austria, to name but a few. I even wrote an article in one of the leading Jewish newspapers. Frankly, I didn't think it would be published, for Jews will tolerate every sort of Jew with the exception of a Messianic one. However, the editor gave me a full-page spread where I was able to make George's plight known.

Then in 1990, I discovered the Rt Hon William Waldegrave was leading a delegation from our Foreign Office

to the Kremlin. Just before they were to leave, I placed before him information concerning George Belitzskie. Instead of ignoring it, Waldegrave wrote to me.

Foreign and Commonwealth Office
London
SW1A 2AH
15th December 1989
From the Minister of State

Dear Mrs. Lockwood,

Thank you for your letter of 22nd November. I am replying as Minister responsible for relations with the Soviet Union.

We have made numerous representations about this case to the Soviet authorities in the past. We will continue to do so until there is a satisfactory outcome (the next major opportunity will be when a delegation of Foreign Office officials meet Deputy Foreign Minister Mr Adamishin on 9-10 January next year in Moscow).

The Hon William Waldegrave.

Less than one month after this meeting George was reunited with his family in Israel, and I have had many invitations to celebrate Passover with him and his family.
'Next year in Jerusalem, George!'

12

How's Your Queen?

Shortly after my husband reached Britain's official retirement age of sixty-five he and I decided it would be good to retire to a cottage near the North Wales coast, not too far from Llandudno, where we'd spent part of our honeymoon, and later enjoyed several short breaks. There we now reside.

Penrallt Baptist Church in Bangor, where the minister was then the Rev Patrick J. Baker, soon became our spiritual home for some seven years. At 8:30 most Saturday mornings, we joined Patrick and a number of the church folk for a prayer meeting. At one of those meetings in 1991, a tall, dark American named Richard Showalter joined us, for he was the visiting guest preacher at both the morning and evening services during the following day.

I had always wanted to visit the United States of America. Somehow, and I don't know quite why, the USA held a fascination for me. I wasn't much interested in Disneyland and the regular tourist trails. I wanted to see small town America; what I saw as the real America.

'So why don't you?' Richard asked, after the evening service. 'Here's my business card ...'

I shrugged. 'Perhaps one day,' I said, with a smile, yet believing I'd never actually go there.

'Many of our Mennonite pastors would be overjoyed to have you testify to congregations. And I'm sure all my students would be enriched.'

'Your students?'

Richard nodded, and explained that he was at that time the President of Rosedale Bible Institute in the small town of Irwin, Ohio. (He has since moved on, and is now the head of the Mennonite Missions, based in Pennsylvania.)

Eric, who had been half listening to the conversation, added that we, as a family, occasionally gave Passover demonstrations, primarily as an object lesson to demonstrate the Last Supper, and how the Christian service of Holy Communion was born from it.

'Hey!' exclaimed Richard. 'That'd be really great! Think about it, you guys.'

Richard explained how Rosedale Bible Institute was a good Mennonite Bible School, born of conviction and empowered by the Holy Spirit, equipping Christians for the ministry.

'But if we did visit, where would we stay?' I began.

'No problem!' Richard exclaimed. 'My wife and I will host you.'

We knew next to nothing about the Mennonites, with the exception they were all pacifists ... 'Peaceful folk.' Eric wondered about what role he would play, how would they accept his testimony, for he came to know the Lord Jesus Christ as his Saviour in 1945, when, as a young soldier, he attended a Gospel meeting in Cairo, convened by the Mission to Mediterranean Garrisons. When he voiced these fears, Richard didn't see it as a problem. 'Just as long as you don't oppose our views on pacifism ...'

'So you're serious about us visiting?'

'Yep. Sure am. Testimonies, Passover Demonstrations ... so many of the Mennonite pastors would want you, not just in Ohio but in New York State, Pennsylvania, Maryland, Indiana

and ...'

I interrupted. 'We'll think and pray about it.'

Drizzling rain hung in the air when we landed in Columbus airport. I suppressed a whoop of joy at just being on American soil. Richard Showalter, that faithful servant of the Lord, was waiting and gave each of us a hug, including eight-year-old Matthew, who was totally jet-lagged. As Richard drove us out of Columbus' busy traffic, through into the flat rural farming land to Rosedale Bible Institute, I began to secretly wonder about Columbus.

Columbus seemed an odd choice of hero for a country which celebrates as America does, because he was such a dismal failure! Consider the facts: he made four wrong voyages to the Americas, but never once realised he wasn't in Asia. While every other explorer brought back new produce like potatoes, all Columbus found to bring home were some puzzled-looking Indians — and he thought they were Japanese. But perhaps Columbus' most remarkable short-coming was that he never actually saw the land which was to become the United States. All his voyages were spent either in the Caribbean or bouncing around the swampy coast of Central America. The Vikings actually discovered America. Yes, they did! Amazing really, for they didn't take any nonsense from anybody, which is the American way!

Just as Richard Showalter had planned, we were based in one of RBI's staff apartments well away from the usual tourist trail, where few locals had ever met any of us Brits in the flesh.

Having settled in the smart, two-bedroomed apartment, we desperately needed to stock up with provisions. Although there were grocery stores in the small towns of nearby Mechanicsburg and Plain City, we decided to make the twelve-mile trip to Kroger's in Urbana.

Many of our out of town supermarkets here in Britain

cannot be regarded as small, with banking services, a post office, a chemist and a café. However, I challenge any to compare ours with the open all hours Kroger's who seemed to have everything we have and much more, not excluding a colourful selection of artificial floral wreaths for a 'do it yourself' funeral.

If there were an Olympic medal for wandering off, my husband would have no problem in obtaining a gold every time. 'Please, Eric, don't leave me here or I'll probably never find you again!' I pleaded, although I might well have been speaking to the proverbial brick wall!

I pushed a huge cart (shopping trolley to the likes of you and me) with the ubiquitous wobbly wheel, up and down seemingly endless aisles and, with the exception of some items such as cornflakes, I was unsure concerning some of my purchases and their prices, hoping we'd brought enough to pay for it all.

Feeling I'd just completed a half marathon, we finally reached the checkout, where the gum-chewing assistant, avoiding all eye contact, informed me in a singsong voice of the cost. Unaccustomed to the local accent, I looked decidedly blank. She'd spoken at such speed, I asked her to repeat herself. It was then she turned to face me full on, squinting suspiciously, as if I was stalling to pay; telling me again. Yet I was none the wiser.

Apologising, I explained that we'd only just arrived in the States, and I neither understood the accent, nor the money. 'See ... here is what I have — please, would you just help yourself?' I asked, opening wide my dollar-stuffed purse, mentally trying to convert it back into sterling.

Grinning full faced at me, the woman's mood switched to becoming overly helpful; monotonously, she counted out each dollar bill and cent, confirming she'd taken the correct amount, warning me not to invite too many folk to just help themselves to the contents!

'Awl the way from England, huh? Hey, howdy like Ohio, then? Oh, wow, I'd sure like t' see your wonderful country, but I'll never find the dough. I bet it's real great there, huh? Oh, and how's yer queen, huh? Living in such a little titchy country, I betcha' get t' see her real often, huh?' she asked, bombarding me with umpteen questions, just as if we'd dropped in from outer space instead of North Wales, which she was sure was in England and a stone's throw from Switzerland!

As we began to leave, she turned and called across to a giggly check-out girl seated at the next till. 'See those guys, huh? They're English.'

Confirming I wasn't deaf, I turned back and smiled at the pair.

'Have a nice day,' they called to me in unison. 'Missing you already!'

Kroger's next-door neighbour was Wal-Mart's jumbo-sized chain store, which made its founder one of the richest men in America. It was a maze of aisles, selling jewellery, leather goods, stationery and clothing, including the brightest of orange bras, plus just about everything you've ever combed the world's high streets for.

It was in this shopaholic's paradise I decided to buy some tights, but the American way of sizing was, to me, a complete enigma. A middle-aged, squat and chunky woman began to stroll mindlessly by. 'Excuse me, please,' I said, stopping her in her tracks. 'Would you advise me? I need to buy ...'

She glowed with pleasure. 'Well, I do declare! England, huh? Hey, I'd sure like to drop in at that Buckingham Palace of your Queen's. By the way, how's she doing these days, huh? And do y' see her real often, then? She speaks real good English, doesn't she?'

Not again! Trying to steer her back to the matter of my tights, and eventually succeeding, she began to chuckle, explaining there'd be no tights to fit me. 'Here in America,

tights are usually thick woolly things for little girls to wear. I think what you want is pantyhose, but we usually just say "hose". Here, look, these should fit you. Hey, and if you bump into your Queen, tell her Miriam Jane Hill says Hi! Okay? Now you really won't forget, will you?'

I smiled at her naivety, half promising to remember.

I turned to speak to Eric, but he was nowhere to be seen. In such a vast shopping scene, I didn't reckon much of my chances of finding him. I trotted up and down, searching almost every aisle, without success. I grabbed at the sleeve of a young assistant's brown overall. He'd just emerged from the stock room, and I explained to him in a flurry of words, that I'd lost my husband.

'Gee, I sure am real sorry about that, lady. When did he die?' he asked sympathetically. 'Was it some sort of an automobile accident? I tell yer, these roads ain't getting no better.' Sombrely, he pointed me back into the direction of Kroger's flower stall, where the wreaths were sold.

'No!' I laughed, 'he just wandered off in this maze, and I can't find him anywhere.'

'Wow, lady, where did you get that amazing accent? You ain't from around these here parts. Britain, eh? Now then ...'

Before he began asking about our Queen, Eric made his appearance, only half-promising not to wander off ever again. Promises are meant to be kept!

Not anxious to spend hours grappling with the cooker, we dumped all our groceries in the kitchen, either in the food cupboards, or the fridge-freezer, and decided to make our way to the town of Plain City, a short drive from Rosedale Bible Institute. Plain City is the home of the Pennsylvanian Dutch, the Amish and the Mennonites.

During our time at RBI, one of the female students teased us that the Mennonites were named after a well-known brand of deodorant, but Mennonite Jewel Showalter, Richard's wife, told us they were named after Menno Simons, one of their

early leaders. In Europe they were called the Anabaptists. They came to America 250 years ago.

The Amish split from the Mennonites in 1693, and there have been countless subdivisions since, but the thing they all have in common is they wear simple clothes; the Amish shun all modern contrivances. That's why the small town was named Plain City.

Many tourists are fascinated by the Amish way of life, by the idea of people living 200 years in the past, so they come in droves to gawk. Every tourist hopes to see and photograph some genuine Amish, a real offence to these people, as they associate photography with the making of graven images, forbidden in the Decalogue.

Many of the Amish themselves have given up and moved out into the countryside, to the back roads, although their distinctive black buggies can often be seen with a long line of cars creeping along behind!

In Plain City we went to the Der Dutchman, one of the many barn-like family-style Amish restaurants. The car park was packed with cars and there were people waiting inside the huge building. Eric and I debated leaving, but a tall fat man told us not to give up because it was well worth the wait.

'The food is that good,' he said, and where food was concerned he'd clearly had some experience!

Eventually, we were ushered into a big dining room, to a clean table quickly prepared for us. Everywhere one looked diners were shovelling food into their mouths, elbows flapping, as if they hadn't eaten for a week.

A young waitress dressed in a starched blue dress started to bring in the food — thick slabs of ham, mountains of fried chicken and 'buckets' of mashed potato, along with all kinds of vegetables.

Just when we felt our stomachs were bulging, she started bringing in large slices of peach pie and bowls of homemade vanilla ice cream. During our meal, we looked up and Janice

Price, the Maitre-D, was showing in Elton Yutzy, one of the pastors from Maranatha Mennonite Church, in Plain City.

Once seated, he removed his baseball cap, and, in obedience to the strong suggestion on the top of each menu, he offered a prayer of thanksgiving for the meal. Replacing his cap, he began to tuck in! This Amish suggestion of saying grace was observed by a group of tall, overweight truckers who joined him at his table.

Full to bursting, we eventually stumbled zombie-like around the adjoining gift shop, with its expensive array of patchwork quilts, beautifully hand crafted by both the Amish and Mennonites — way outside our budget!

We got into the car, borrowed from Jewel, too full to speak, and headed towards the greenish glow of RBI, where a student offered us a bucket of popcorn!

Never say 'thank you' in America.

We went into the bank, and made the mistake of saying thank you.

'You're welcome,' said the bank clerk. 'Have a nice day.'

'Thank you.'

'You're welcome!'

There was no stopping it!

The Post Office, a few doors along, was no different. I asked for some stamps.

'There you go,' said the clerk.

'Thank you,' I replied.

'You're welcome,' she answered.

There are some lovely folk, Salina and Albert Eberly, who then had the apartment below ours, and I hope when I arrive in heaven, my mansion is right next door to theirs! Salina asked if we'd spend part of Good Friday fellowshipping with them.

'Thank you, that'd be great,' I replied. 'Thank you very much.'

'You're welcome,' she said.

The next day we called in to fill up our car with petrol at the gas station in nearby Mechanicsburg, a small town which, compared with busy Columbus, should have been named 'Coma'. The nineteen-year-old man sitting behind the till was also fascinated by our British accent, promising himself to one day visit our little ol' country.

'Is your English money different to ours?' he asked, introducing himself as William.

I nodded, and gave him some of our small change: a fifty pence piece, and so on.

He was pleased. 'Why are you over here?'

I explained our reasons, and how we were based at Rosedale. 'If you would like to call in at our apartment sometime, we'd be very pleased to see you, William.'

He took me at my word, and one evening, he turned up with a couple of large pizzas! He also came to one of our Passover demonstrations at the nearby Mechanicsburg Mennonite Church.

The Passover is one of the miraculous events of Jewish history. It commemorates the passing of the Angel of Death over those homes which had their lintels and doorposts sprinkled with the sacrificial blood, without injury to those within; whereas, in those homes where God's instruction was not obeyed, the firstborn of the family died. Secondly, it was a perpetual reminder of the deliverance of Israel, out of their bondage in Egypt. It is, therefore, a day of thanksgiving and joy.

This festival is also known as the Feast of Unleavened Bread, and it lasts from the 15th to the 22nd of Nisan (see Exodus 13:3-10). The Passover, or Seder Service, as it is called, begins with the return of the head of the family from

the synagogue.

We set out a table in front of the Mechanicsburg Mennonite congregation. On the table was placed an egg and three slices of unleavened bread (matzos) hidden in a napkin. The matzos are flat biscuits, like water biscuits, but larger.

Beside those, I set a bowl of salt water, which was intended to represent the tears of affliction shed in the land of bondage. There was also a bunch of parsley, in lieu of hyssop, and some horseradish as a reminder of the bitterness of slavery. Finally, a mixture called Haroseth, which was composed of almonds, dates, apples and nuts, to represent the clay from which the bricks were made in Egypt. Four cups of wine symbolised the four promises made in Exodus 6:6-7, 'I will bring you out', 'I will rid you', 'I will redeem you', and 'I will take you to me'.

The Passover story is set forth in Exodus 12. At this point in the talk, I stressed the spiritual significance of the feast, for in verse 13, God said, *'When I see the blood, I will pass over you'*. This is important, since no lamb is slain at the Passover service nowadays. Instead, there is placed on the table, the burnt shank of a lamb, for God did not say, 'when I see your good works', or 'when I see how well you keep the law'. No. He said, *'When I see the blood, I will pass over you'*.

I reminded the congregation of what Isaiah, the prophet had written (Isaiah 53:6), *'We all, like sheep, have gone astray, each of us has turned to his old way; and the Lord has laid upon him the iniquity of us all.'* This method of sacrifice runs right through the Tenach — the Old Testament — and is continued until the New Testament, where it finds its fulfilment and completion in the Lord Jesus Christ. John the Baptist summed it all up when he said, *'Look, the Lamb of God, who takes away the sin of the world!'* (John 1:29).

'So,' spoke up one of the congregation, 'it's not only the Jews who have rejected the only way of salvation, but Gentiles, too?'

I nodded. 'It's true. Passover not only brings us all to remember a deliverance from physical bondage, but the sacrifice of Jesus Christ for the sins of the world, a deliverance from the bondage and tyranny of sin. (Hebrews 2:15.)

After the Passover demonstration, the Pastor stood up and said that those who wished to be assured of their eternal salvation must accept God's way, which would be their only safeguard; it must be by accepting the sacrifice, which the Lord had provided at such infinite cost.

So I gave out an appeal. 'What will your choice be? Remember the consequences are eternal. Do not act rashly. Think first, and carefully. By accepting God's way of salvation, you have everything to gain — pardon from your sin; peace with God; power to live a new life, and, one day, the privilege of living in His presence for eternity.'

William listened.

13

A Soldier Saved

Most Thursday evenings we, along with some of the college faculty of Rosedale Bible College and a few of the students, went to the Showalters' home for supper. It was situated a mile or so from the college where Richard Showalter was then president. It was during one of those times when he approached me regarding our presenting a demonstration Passover to all the students and most of the staff.

'Hey-y-y-y! It'd be great if you guys could combine it with a lunchtime meal in the college refectory,' he said. 'I know Sarah will give her testimony, but it would sure be good to hear yours, Eric.'

Eric hesitated, for he was saved during his time as a young soldier in the British Army, and, knowing those to whom he'd be speaking were all pacifists, he felt he just might upset the apple cart, as it were.

Richard shook his head. 'It'll be just fine, brother. Just you go ahead and tell us how the Lord broke into your life.'

The day came. The college's cooks, Loretta Wagler and Miriam Jantzi worked hard the whole morning. Having spread Cambridge blue tablecloths over ten long trestle tables, they laid out the very best crockery and cutlery; the crystal

glasses sparkled like the sun through a prism.

'My, it looks like a wedding reception!' I declared, as Miriam polished up the silver candlesticks, one for each table.

'Mm ... the food smells good!' exclaimed Matthew who'd trailed in behind me.

'You can smell the lamb casserole,' she replied. 'It will be accompanied by a side salad.'

'Yes, and everyone will have red grape juice as a drink,' added Loretta. 'We'll have to keep a close eye on the male students — they'd drink the whole lot, given half a chance!'

By noon, staff and students began to file in and, once the president had said grace, everyone tucked into the fine food; the male students attempting to consume the lion's share. Anything the female students left was speared away by the men! Empty plates and full stomachs gave way to the proceedings.

After I'd finished my testimony, the Passover began just as we'd performed many times in the past, except on this particular afternoon we brought out the importance of the four cups of wine used at certain points during the demonstration; how this historic occasion was based on Exodus 2:24-25, where God made four promises to the enslaved Hebrews: 'I will bring you out; I will rescue you; I will redeem you; I will take you.' The four cups illustrating those promises are named:

1.   The cup of sanctification

2.   The cup of telling forth

3.   The cup of blessing and redemption

4.   The cup of completion

All those sharing in the celebration drank from a cup at

the appropriate place in the demonstration. It was thrilling to be able to tell them, as they drank from the cup of blessing and redemption, how our actual goblet on the Passover table was given to me by an Orthodox Jewish rabbi who confided that he did secretly believe that Jesus was the Messiah, but, scared for his life, he didn't dare declare it.

As Eric stood to his feet, he testified:

Home, during the early years of my life, was in the foothills of the Yorkshire Pennines. The road from the industrial town of Huddersfield winds south through the Holme Valley towards the moorland area called Holme Moss. The stupendous panorama from this high point stretches as far as the eye can see. The valley bottom is the location of many textile mills with their tall, Victorian chimneys reaching up into the sky. The slopes of the valley are a patchwork of grassy fields enclosed within blackened dry stone walls; higher still are the uncultivated moorlands, magnificent to behold in late summer when patches of heather turn purple.

My parents, hard-working responsible folk, were both employees in the fine worsted textile industry but, when they started a family, Mum resigned. She certainly had more than enough to do at home!

I was the second son in their family of four. From about the age of twelve, my great ambition was to one day become a carpenter. Nearly every Saturday morning found me scurrying off to the joiner's shop in Hinchliffe Mill, spending what little pocket money I had on off-cuts of wood. Even the very smell of wood in the place was, for me, intoxicating. However, as we were not a very well-off family, a three year apprenticeship to train as a joiner was out of the question; so, on leaving school at fourteen, I became a wage earner in the same textile factory, to help balance the family budget.

At a bend in the narrow road, winding up the hillside into

a hamlet known as Austonley, there stood a small stone building — Hall Sunday School, built by public subscription sometime during the middle of the nineteenth century, to serve the needs of children in the locality.

How vividly I remember those Sunday afternoons, sitting on one of the wooden benches, having to read round from an unattractive old black Bible and giggling together with the other kids over a passage from the book of Kings which we children thought was a bit saucy.

For some reason, I don't remember a single thing the Sunday school teachers were trying to get across, except the verses from one of the hymns we used to sing from the Methodist Hymn Book which stuck in my mind:

> In loving kindness Jesus came,
> My soul in mercy to reclaim,
> And from the depths of sin and shame
> Through grace he lifted me.
>
> From sinking sand he lifted me;
> With tender hand he lifted me;
> From shades of night to plains of light,
> O praise his name, he lifted me.

Probably about ten years passed before the words of that hymn became true for me. I had joined the regular army. On my way home from the recruiting office I met my father in the lane leading up to the smallholding adjoining our home. After informing him as to where I'd been and what I'd done, he stopped in his tracks and stared at me in his serious way: 'You've made your bed, lad, so now you must lie on it!' With that, he walked ahead, virtually leaving me standing.

At the time God began to make His presence felt in my life, I was serving with an army unit in the Middle East. Nearby was a Soldiers' Home where there were facilities for

either playing games or writing letters home. There was also an excellent canteen — a welcome change from army food! This refuge from army life was run by a group of Christians from the Missions to Military Garrisons, and most of its workers then were women.

Passing through the doors of the Soldiers' Home, an army colleague led the way up a flight of stone steps. Standing at the top of the landing was a tall, thin, middle-aged woman. Her name was Elsie M. Potter; one of the team of women who served among service personnel in many of the garrison towns of the Middle East. She had no time for any customary small talk in which people often engage when they first meet. Noticing the lighted cigarette in my hand, she threw down the gauntlet — a challenge I was definitely not expecting! 'Young man, what will you have with that cigarette when you have finished it?' she asked, her eyes firmly fixed upon mine.

'Nothing,' I sheepishly replied.

'Oh yes you will! You will have ashes, and what will you have with your life when it is finished, eh?'

To Elsie Potter's challenge I made no response.

It was part of the routine in the Soldiers' Home to finish the day with a brief gospel meeting. Although it was not obligatory, the soldiers were actively encouraged to attend. I went along, not knowing quite what it was all about. In the afterglow of the service, I was buttonholed by two or three Christians who were seated near me. Resisting the arguments of those zealous believers, I informed them I was a Communist and made a rapid escape! All I remember from the evening meeting was a name — the name of Jesus Christ.

When I returned to the camp the barrack room was totally deserted. Pondering over the events of the evening, so different, I was aware how, deep down within me, there was a real need for something, or someone. Although I had lived for twenty years in a so-called Christian country and attended a

Sunday school as a child, I still did not even know the real meaning of Christmas, Good Friday, or Easter Day.

Alone, I knelt down beside my army bed and asked my then "unknown" Lord Jesus Christ to be my saviour. There was no blinding flash of light; however, a few days later I was conscious of a sudden upsurge of joy as I became aware of something new and wonderful happening in my life.

During that skirmish with Christians in the Soldiers' Home, someone had given me a khaki-coloured New Testament which also contained the book of Psalms. This book became alive for me in a most powerful way: God used Psalm 91 to bring me through a worrying and strange experience of an almost indefinable fear. Prior to service in the Middle East, I was involved as an infantryman in the invasion of north-west Europe. The trauma of this left me with a legacy of fear which was at its worst during the hours of darkness. Night after night I would drop to my knees beside my bed and seek God's presence, using the words of Psalm 91, verses 1 and 2:

> He who dwells in the shelter of the Most
> High will rest in the shadow of the Almighty.
> I will say of the Lord, He is my refuge and
> my fortress, my God, in whom I trust.

Time and time again the oppression lifted and the fear departed — eventually forever. I find it almost impossible to fully convey the way this Psalm underpinned my life, giving me confidence and a sense of security.

Many years later, a study of Psalm 91 revealed to me the opening verses which contain four of the most powerful Hebrew names of the living God: Elohim, Elyon, El-Shaddai, and Yahweh.

At the same time all of this was happening, another scripture was challenging me: the words of Jesus to

Nicodemus. 'I tell you the truth, no-one can see the kingdom of God unless he is born again.' (John 3, verse 3) This verse fascinated me. One Sunday, making my way to the garrison church in Tripoli, I said to myself, 'I do hope someone will speak on the new birth tonight.' Dr J. Lilley, who was a missionary to the Arab community, opened his Bible and gave out the text: 'Except a man be born again be cannot see the kingdom of God.' How thrilling, because / knew it had happened for me! The verse of the hymn we used to sing at Hall Sunday School had come true:

> Now on a higher plane I dwell,
> And with my soul I know 'tis well,
> Yet how or why, I cannot tell,
> He should have lifted me.

Elsie M. Potter was not only a fearless evangelist, but a caring and faithful "shepherdess". Rejoicing at what had happened in my life, she regularly posted me letters of counsel and encouragement to wherever the army sent me. Behind those letters were the powerful prayers of that astonishing Christian saint.

The last year of my military service was spent at a Command Supply Depot in Sudbrook Park, rural Lincolnshire, where I found plenty of time to study God's word and give attention to reading. Over the five years since becoming a Christian, burning within me was the desire to serve the Lord in some sort of preaching ministry.

Living across the road from our army camp was a Methodist preacher, named Fenton Sharpe, who used to take me with him when he conducted worship in the little village chapels, not far from the depot. It was he who encouraged me to apply to Derbyshire's Cliff College, a Methodist Training College for evangelists. There I would prepare myself for whatever God might have in store for me.

Everything seemed to be going swimmingly well. My plans were made, for I'd been accepted as a student at Cliff College, starting in the autumn of 1951; the end of my military service was in sight! Then the blow fell. There was trouble in the Far East. North and South Korea were in conflict. China, America, and the United Kingdom became involved. Demobilisation for British servicemen was cancelled; reservists were recalled from civilian life and an army brigade was formed to serve with the United Nations Task Force. A troopship, which took nearly a month to sail to Korea, was crammed full of disgruntled, discontented troops whose lives had been rudely interrupted. I was one of them!

One of my favourite passages in the Bible was then Psalm 37, verse 23: 'The steps of a good man are ordered by the Lord and he delighteth in his way.' However, we don't always take it kindly when the Sovereign Lord interrupts our plans and disturbs our lives in this way, do we?

Although the bottom seemed to have fallen out of my world, with hindsight I wouldn't have missed it for anything. The lessons learned then, and the adventure of it all were experiences which couldn't have been imparted through academic pursuits. Who would have missed the privilege of meeting with Korean believers in their own country? This land, which boasts today of having some of the largest congregations in the Christian world, had known revival blessings during the years before we arrived in 1950.

Disembarking at Pusan, in southern Korea, we travelled north to the town of Taegu where we were billeted in a public building requisitioned for military use. The evenings were long and there was little to do except sit around a very effective oil-burning stove of American design, chatting or reading. There was no TV, radio, cinema, or any organised entertainment. Seeking Christian fellowship, 1 discovered a Presbyterian church nearby and, although I was unable to speak a word of Korean, I started to attend the services.

After a few weeks of sitting on the rush matting with the rest of the congregation, I was taken aback one evening when some men staggered into the church carrying a big armchair for my use. I didn't really want it, but to avoid offence, sat in it. They must have thought it inappropriate for a western brother to sit cross-legged on the floor!

A bigger shock came when they asked me to speak. At that time I was unaccustomed to public speaking, having only given my testimony once or twice. However, I told them about the church back home, and what the Lord was doing there. How the interpreter coped with my Yorkshire accent and hesitating speech, goodness alone knows, but he did very well, saying much more than I had seemed to say!

The crowning shock came when the interpreter declared: 'Now we are ready for your solo ...'

How could I explain to him that the talents of Ira D. Sankey had not been given to me? Launching into the gospel song, 'Jesus keep me near the cross' I was delighted when they at least recognised the tune and joined their beautiful voices in singing the refrain. 'In the cross, in the cross, be my glory ever.' East and west were joined together in recognition of the mighty love of God seen in the cross of Christ. Over the years I've had the great privilege of leading worship many times, but never once has that Moody and Sankey act been repeated!

The transfer of our army unit from Korea to Kure, Japan, was a welcome surprise, giving rise to further Christian growth, with opportunities for me to witness. The joy of meeting three other Christian fellows, Austin Martin, Bill Clayton, and Ernest Potter, was a cordial to my spirit. Together, we spent our off duty hours in the hills overlooking Kure Harbour, engaged in amateur photography, and just simply getting to know one another. Each evening, almost without exception, we met around the harmonium in a hospital chapel. Although we were without experienced

leadership, we sang, shared, read the Bible and prayed. Great days!

The group of us started up a Christian meeting in the Salvation Army citadel which a handful of Japanese high school youngsters attended. We were very inexperienced, and must have made multitudes of mistakes in our cross-cultural exchanges, but the Lord undertook for us.

The crowning joy for me was being befriended by Mr Takashi Horioka, a Japanese schoolmaster who taught English in a high school. Welcoming us into his home, he also invited us to go on family picnics and sometimes to even eat with the children from his school.

He showed an interest in the Christian way, so I loaned him a book written by C. H. Spurgeon on the subject of salvation. He returned it with the words: 'I am a sinner.' That is as far as he seemed to go. I had to just simply commit him to God, leaving it with Him.

After my return to the UK, I corresponded with Mr Horioka on a number of occasions. He made little mention of spiritual things, although in one letter he wrote: 'The happy times we had together come back to my mind vividly. I have come to understand Englishmen and am deeply moved by your faith.'

The year following life's rude interruption of my plans, the army released me to attend Cliff College. I stayed three years, first as a student and then as a member of the evangelistic staff.

The pattern of my life thereafter was as one serving the Lord within the capacity of a Methodist preacher.

However, another of life's wonderful surprises surfaced when I met Sarah after an evening service in a Methodist church near Huddersfield, West Yorkshire. A friendship was formed, love developed, and the following year we were married. Our youngest son, Matthew, was born in 1984, and here at the time I am talking to you, he is sitting beside me.

Whatever the future holds for us, God is unchanging and I look back with thanksgiving to the time when 'From sinking sand he lifted me.'

At the close of Eric's testimony, he challenged the Rosedale students as to how their faith had affected others since they'd first believed. Some were quiet and thoughtful.

14

Off at the Ramp

'**I** wish I could see Niagara Falls, Eric,' I told my husband. 'It seems such a shame to have come all this way without seeing them.'

'So why don't you?' suggested Richard helpfully. 'It shouldn't be more than an eight or nine hours' drive.'

I stared at him in disbelief. 'How long?' I gasped.

Richard shrugged. 'It's nothing. The trouble with you Brits is that you have island mentality!' he said. 'Hey, why don't you combine it with some ministry in one of the Mennonite churches in New York State. My good friend, Titus Kaufman, is a pastor not too far from Niagara, at a place called Alden.'

Getting out his road map, Richard showed the two of us how we would need to travel up to New York State, where Niagara was situated, some 600 miles from New York.

'You need to get onto the interstate, which circles Columbus, and then come off at the ramp, at Exit 71 North. You'll be first heading to Cleveland.'

Two days later, Eric and I were on our way. Matthew, our son, then eight years old, was seated in the back of our hired car; a brand new white Dodge.

'Richard said to look for the ramp,' I reminded Eric,

presuming a ramp meant road works with a dip in the surfacing.

'Well, there doesn't appear to be any,' Eric said, as he drove along the interstate.

'We've been round this way already,' Matthew piped up. 'I've seen those billboards before.'

Suddenly we swept off with the traffic like a cork on a fast-moving river. Instead of coming off the interstate towards Cleveland, we were circling Columbus, and the whole journey was becoming laden with frustration. The highway authorities in Ohio had been reluctant to impart much in the way of useful signs, like the road we were actually on. All we knew was that we were on a six lane intersection with twelve traffic lights, all with arrows pointing this way and that; 71 North seemed to have been hidden somewhere else.

To put it tactfully, Eric was totally cheesed off. With an inane desire to be geographically orientated, he pulled up in a parking lot and asked someone the way.

'Hey, don't you guys worry about a thing,' the stranger began, and offered to drive ahead of us, explaining that a ramp was just an exit off — nothing to do with road works!

Finally, with light hearts, we were siphoned off, heading in the right direction.

Matthew's heart, however, was anything but light! He too was also cheesed off, driving us up the wall by repeatedly asking those familiar words known to all parents: 'Are we nearly there yet? When are we going to get there? I'm bored. I feel sick! I've got nothing to do!'

We arrived in the small town of Niagara, but we couldn't locate the Falls.

'I'm sure we aren't too far away now,' I said, peering at a road map again.

'Maybe we should stop and ask some passers-by,' Matthew suggested.

Eric agreed. In fact, by then he was agreeing to anything!

From some open window high up came the sound of a stereo turned up too loud. Then came a booming voice, which stated; 'If you don't turn that thing off right now, I'm gonna come over and pound your head in!'

The music stopped.

Seeing two very overly made up women walking arm in arm, Eric asked them how far it was to the Falls. 'Can you direct us?'

Instead of them saying, 'Sure we can', he got: 'We ain't gettin' in no car with you, mister!' from the red-headed one with the beehive hairstyle, who'd somehow managed to pour her capacious body into some black leggings and tight green jacket, as if she'd dressed in her granddaughter's clothes by mistake.

'All I want you to do is to please give me directions to Niagara Falls.'

'You ain't no pimp, then?' asked the second, squinting at him through bright blue-framed spectacles.

'Of course not! My wife, my son and I simply want to go and see Niagara Falls,' he stated slowly and indignantly. After the long drive, the man was "done in"!

'It's that way,' they replied in unison, flaying their arms about.

'Do I look like a pimp?' Eric bristled, on returning to the car and slamming the door.

'I dunno!' I laughed, appreciatively. 'What does a pimp look like?'

Nothing prepared me for Niagara. No matter how much I'd heard about it or seen pictures, it just took my breath away as it tumbled noisily down in the bright spring sunshine. My mind, unable to deal with anything on that scale, couldn't believe anything on God's earth could be so vast, so beautiful.

Even Matthew was stilled by it. It was probably the only

occasion in all that time he had stopped talking, apart from short breaks for sleeping.

I became aware of a vaguely irritating noise beside me. It was a beefy, white haired Canadian with a video camera, with all kinds of power packs and auxiliary paraphernalia strapped to his body. The camera was enormous; it must have been like going on holiday with a vacuum cleaner! He looked exhausted, but he was determined to film every drop of water issuing from Niagara Falls, even at the risk of acquiring a hernia! What he hadn't noticed was that his young grandson was just about to climb through the rails, which prevented the rest of us ending up in a watery grave. My gasp and Matthew's shout made him look away from his lens just in time to see the toddler.

Back in the car, I asked Eric to please drive the very short distance across to one of the souvenir shops, but he replied he would find it too difficult.

'It's not like driving on the roads at home, where everything is second nature to me. Now I really have to think carefully. I'm on the "wrong" side of the road here,' he said, the veins in his forehead lively, aware of being in charge of a ton of speeding metal.

'But all the rest of the traffic is on the wrong side of the road, too!' I argued with a decidedly limited acuity, staring out at the lonesome, three dimensional billboards, thirty feet wide, and fifteen feet high, which was about the only visual stimulation I was going to get. One said, 'Amish restaurant just 106 miles'; another said: 'Shape up with Shell'. I had to leave Eric with it, like a pilot making passes over an unfamiliar airport.

Turning on the car radio and twirling the dial, I heard the news, which lasted about 30 seconds: 'On Wall Street today, April 1st, shares had their biggest one day fall in history, losing 508 points in just three hours. And the weather outlook for Springfield, Ohio ... clear skies, becoming cloudy later,

with a two percent chance of precipitation.

'You're listening, as it happens, to radio Springfield, where you get up to the minute news on the hour, every hour.'

I was amazed ... the American economy in shreds? A new great depression?

And then I remembered the day — April 1st!

We needed some petrol, and so we pulled up at a gas station by the side of the then frozen southern shoreline of Lake Erie. It is impossible to exaggerate the immensity of the Great Lakes. There are five of them, Erie, Huron, Michigan, Superior and Ontario; and God made them all! They stretched 700 miles from top to bottom, 900 miles from east to west. They covered 94,500 square miles, making them almost the precise size of the United Kingdom. Together they form the largest expanse of fresh water on earth. Fantastic, eh?

We drove through the thin light of the afternoon. The weather in Alden was unbelievably cold. There was ice and snow on the pavements, yet there was something uncommonly alluring about the day. We had left behind the start of the Welsh spring, where trees were in blossom, daffodils in full bloom, and lawn mowers were coming out of the winter storage. In Alden it seemed we had stepped back in time, where the sense of winter was drawing in, and we were in the extreme cold of the North American winter. By four o'clock, the daylight had gone. Any glimmer of sunlight had dropped behind the distant houses like a coin into a piggy bank. It was flat, too. If we'd stood on two phone directories, we'd probably have had a really good view! It was a quiet town.

Skis were propped by the Kaufmans' front door. Brilliantly colourful wild birds were pecking around, searching for scraps. The house, built from felled lumber by Titus, was beautiful inside and out. I was seized with a huge 'envy' for these Mennonites and their unassuming lives.

They claimed it was good to live in a safe and timeless place, where one knows everyone and everyone knows you, and one can count on each other, where crime rarely exists in such a place.

It was not until our arrival that we discovered Barbara Kaufman, having fallen on the ice a month previously, had suffered a fractured wrist. Her hand and forearm were still in plaster.

'You should have told us you'd hurt your wrist. We wouldn't have stayed here had we known,' I said.

'Why ever not?' Titus asked. 'Does it offend you?'

Eric shook his head. 'What Sarah meant was that we don't wish to be an added burden,' he began.

'Nonsense! It's just good for Barbara and me to have you as our guests.'

Eric and I couldn't not love the Kaufmans and it was evident that God was using Titus as the overseer of the Mennonite circuit in Alden, where there were fast-growing evangelical places of worship.

The Benders, a middle-aged couple who were elders in the Alden church, asked Titus if we could spend most of the Sunday with them. They took us to the church services before feeding us with a grand blow-out of a chicken for lunch. Afterwards they filled much of the afternoon showing us their large bookstore and bakery. From Monday to Saturday pies and bread were baked and sold, including my dietary downfall — peach pie! Mrs Bender, finding a couple of the fruit pies, carved off large slices for us all. She didn't want us to attend the evening service on an empty stomach.

When it was time to leave for church, Eric and Matthew made their way towards our hired car. I stepped out on what I thought was flat ground. Instead, I took a tumble down some unlit steps. Feeling embarrassed, I quickly scrambled to my feet, assuring the Benders I was okay.

Once in the car, Eric asked how I was. He wondered if I

would manage to stand during the evening service. It had been planned by Titus that I should give my testimony.

Next morning when I tried to put my foot on the floor, I gave a squeal. My foot was now badly bruised and very swollen.

'Don't you think it should be seen by a doctor?' Eric asked. 'It could be fractured.'

Thankfully it wasn't.

After we had arrived back in Wales, I received an enigmatic telephone call from New York. The male caller, a consultant psychiatrist in his early fifties, had been passing through Alden. By 'chance' he decided to drop in at the Mennonite church. After hearing my testimony, he drove to his apartment. There, much to his wife's amazement, he knelt and surrendered his life to the Lord.

What amazing providence! And how blessed we felt to know that our long journey to that small town church, not far from the Canadian border, and the 600 miles of motoring by this eminent man from the ever waking city of New York, had culminated in something as wonderful as his salvation.

15

Turkey Run

Before we had left for the USA, a nursing colleague of mine informed me that the eastern side of the United States was nothing but maple trees, white churches and old guys in check jackets sitting around the country general stores and spitting out chewed-up bits of tobacco. However, if the places we had visited, even those with strange-sounding names such as Sugar Creek, Walnut Creek, Apple Creek, Light in the Valley, and Buckeye were considered as evidence, clearly I had been misinformed. Sure, every once in a while there would be a white church, house or barn, yet there was quite a lot of commercial congestion with gas stations and shopping centres standing incongruously in the midst of drive-thru banks, burger joints and motels. Nothing as she had led me to believe.

We had joined an old route, intending to follow the local road right through to Turkey Run, an instantly forgettable little town near Logan, south-eastern Ohio, where we'd hoped it would retain something of country charm; and I suppose it was so, despite the chill of the morning drizzle as seen through the rhythmic swish of windscreen wipers. The road ran for 75 miles from Rosedale to the snug farm nestled in a fold of a hill belonging to Carl and Leota Wesselhoeft.

After about half an hour of travelling when, according to the map, we seemed to have moved only a remarkably tiny distance, Matthew decided he was starving, so after trying to fill up with petrol at what we discovered was a disused gas station in a singular lack of picturesqueness, we crossed over to a little café which claimed to be 'The friendliest place in town'. The woman at the cash register nodded in the direction of a clean table. The waitress, a plump and dimpled woman, brought a menu. Before we had a chance to read it she rhythmically tapped her pencil on a pad.

'Yo ready to order?' she asked.

'Please, give us a few moments,' I said.

She shrugged and returned with a cloth to wipe the already clean table. 'Ready to order yet?'

'No, not quite.'

'Yo wanna ashtray?'

'No, thank you. We don't smoke.'

'Please yerselves. Yo want some iced water? I'll bring y' some. I'll bring some cutlery, too.'

'Thank you.'

'You're welcome,' she droned mindlessly.

We ordered the 'fried breakfast special'. As we waited we became uncomfortably aware that the folk at the next table were watching and smiling at us in a deranged fashion. The waitress was also watching from a position by the kitchen doorway. It was all rather unnerving.

Eventually the waitress set down the plates of food in front of us. 'Yo want some ketchup?'

We didn't.

'What about some coffee?'

'Really, we're fine ... maybe a little later. Thank you,' I replied.

Still the people at the next table watched us; they closely watched us eat and smiled. I'd had enough, and from our table I spoke to them — something about the weather, just as

we Brits do. They nodded and the larger of the two men began to ask me about my accent and wanted to know about 'little ol' England', as if we were a race of interplanetary creatures from the Planet Zog, ready to take over Earth.

The waitress listened to the brief conversation and then, so that she could hear better, offered us dessert after our breakfast!

'How about a piece of pie? We got apple pie, peach pie, blueberry pie, huckleberry and cherry pie.'

Eric looked at Matthew and me, and then said, 'No thanks, we're full.'

'Well, what about some ice cream? We got chocolate chip, fudge, mint, chocolate ... that'll be chocolate without the chips ... how about a slice of cake? We got ...'

'Really, no thank you; just some coffee for my wife and me. Our young son would like some milk. That's all.'

'Yo sure?'

'Yes, thank you.'

Never my policy to visit someone empty handed, I decided to look out for a florist, but in small town America there seemed to be a dearth of flower sellers. Just outside Logan we stumbled across a small garden centre, which only sold plants and seeds.

'I have this sort of house plant already in bloom with a pink type of flower,' the owner said.

It looked like a tall fly catcher out of a Hitchcock horror film that would come out and gobble you up in your sleep.

'It's a lily,' I replied, careful not to step back into a small pile of horse manure.

'So, do you want it?'

I nodded. 'But why don't you sell bunches of fresh flowers?'

He eyed me with a dull boredom. 'Why ma'am, there ain't much call for flowers in these parts. Folks around 'ere grow what they want, see. And what do they want with

121

flowers anyway? After all, folks can't eat flowers, can they!' he sniffed.

'Perhaps I should have bought some chocolates instead.'

'Well, there you have it!' he answered. 'Git her sumpin to make her fat.'

Having left the garden centre with the murderous lily for Leota Wesselhoeft, we passed a family of Amish busily turning over the soil in their front garden. On seeing us, the whole family put down their implements and waved for all they were worth. When we saw Amish before, they had seemed to want to ignore us, probably in case we brought the 'world' into their community ... or so they thought.

The weather had changed and the sky was full of those big fluffy clouds you'd see in nautical paintings. The sun was soon high and warm, though a zephyr wind teased through our hair.

Just before the evening meal, Leota took us to the edge of their land so we could meet her elderly mother; a grand old lady living alone in a small white house with green shutters. Carl had built it for her.

Eric sat down beside her, taking her hand in his. 'Don't you ever feel a little lonely, even though most of your family aren't too far away?'

'Lonely? How can I ever be lonely when the Lord chats with me all day long? One day I shall sit and talk with Him face to face ... won't that be grand, Eric?'

Walking back, we saw a rooster sitting like an obelisk on a fence next to the hen hut. Matthew made Leota smile, for he informed her about a pastor named Elton Yutzy who we'd briefly met during our travels. Elton had told Matthew there were rooster eggs in Ohio! Matthew had almost fallen for the joke.

'See, up there?' Leota said, pointing high up the rolling hillside which was fat and soft like a sleeping animal. 'That's our oil well. It's not real big, but it provides just enough fuel

for us. Lots of farming folk around here pump their own oil from the crest of the hill.'

As we walked back to the house I decided to share my fears with Leota. 'I don't wish to say the wrong thing, not in your husband's church. With him being German ... and me being Jewish ... and my dad has been in Auschwitz.'

She threw her head back and laughed. 'You need to hear Carl's testimony — then you'll have no worries. After supper I'll have him tell you the whole story.'

The story Carl Wesselhoeft had to tell of God's protection and providence in his life was so special, I consider it should be told in his own words:

God's protection and providence ran like a thread through my life even before I came to a living faith in Him through our Lord Jesus Christ. As I reflect upon this, I am filled with gratitude and praise to Him who alone is worthy.

I was born in Rostock, Germany, in 1929 and soon afterwards was christened as an infant at the Lutheran church of which my parents were nominal members. Rarely did we attend church, not even for Easter or Christmas.

My growing up experiences were greatly influenced by the rule of the Nazis during World War II. I remember quite vividly a day in 1938, as I made my way to school, how a number of stores in Bostock had their windows broken; merchandise littered the streets. Jewish stores were being looted. In the afternoon, on my way home, I saw fire engines and smoke rising from the synagogue, which had been set on fire. It was not until a few years later that my mother told me, in secret, how we couldn't have anything to do with Nazism because we were unable to prove Aryan descent. It had come to light that my paternal grandmother was a Jewess. This news made me rebellious and I began to secretly listen to the German service of the BBC with my ears glued to the receiving set; such listening was strictly forbidden.

In 1944 I was confirmed in the Lutheran Church, yet I had no clear concept of what it really meant to be a Christian. Shortly after, all the boys in my class were taken into the assembly hall, where each of us was taken aside and asked in which part of the armed forces we were going to serve. Although only fourteen, I volunteered for an armoured unit notwithstanding the pressure upon us to join the SS, an elite corps which, more than the rest of the military, was solidly Nazi in both philosophy and practice. I refused on the basis of my Christian faith because I'd heard that members of the SS had to leave the Church. The interrogator asked me: 'Is it because of your faith or your parents' faith?' I told him it was because of my faith! He continued to pressure me until I eventually told him I would be ready to die for my country, but not in the SS.

At sixteen, the likelihood of my being called to military duty steadily increased, and since my brother was already missing in action (he never returned) my father thought it was wise that I should leave home to avoid a call-up. I left home two weeks before the war ended, and my call-up to the armed forces came one week before that!

With the end of the war a difficult time came, not just for Germany, but for me as a teenager. With disillusionment and anger in my heart, I knew we Germans had been lied to and misled. We had been asked to give our lives for the sacred cause of our country; it had turned into one blatant falsehood. The institution that had failed was the Church. It should have raised its voice against all the madness which had occurred; instead it had been too often the willing handmaid of the State. So, when I had to go through the denazification procedure and fill in the form regarding my church affiliation, I left it blank. The stern clerk, unbending in his rules, stated I could not do that since I had to be 'something'. I'd been christened and confirmed, therefore, on that basis, willingly or not, I had a church affiliation! Reluctantly I completed the

form, yet it held no relevance in my life. The Church seemed to be only for the passages of life: for the hatches, matches and dispatches!

Earlier, while the war was still going on, due to the limitation of public transport because of scarcity of petrol, I could not be driven to school every day. Dad arranged for me to board with another family; they were strangers who lived nearer to the school. Immature for my age, I keenly felt the loss of intimacy of my family. My only brother died in a prison camp in Siberia. My sisters were at boarding schools, and I could only go home during the school holidays. (Even now, as I tell you this, some 54 years later, I can still feel the heaviness which overcame me when I had to leave home again.) In a world that was falling apart, school seemed a waste of time. There were terrifying air raids on Rostock. One night a few British bombs fell, one destroying a neighbour's house. The next night the entire sky became a brilliant red as the whole city burned. Dad sent the horse and wagon to free me from the smouldering place. The following night the house where I should have been scored a direct hit; my school was burnt to a cinder. Naturally my school work suffered — even after the war it didn't improve and I left without completing a secondary education; I became a farmhand. Surprisingly the daily regime of working in the fields became a healing experience. Truly, God had protected me, although I didn't yet know Him.

Everything stagnated in Germany and the interest to search for opportunities abroad became great. An overseas opening presented itself when I obtained a year's work on a farm in Sweden. From there I answered an ad offering farm work in Canada. I left Sweden, went back to visit my parents in Germany, and then I caught the train through to Holland. The ferry took me across the Channel to Dover. I couldn't resist London's tourist attractions — I saw Trafalgar Square, Big Ben, and the Houses of Parliament ... oh and Buckingham

Palace. From Liverpool I caught the ship which would take me to Halifax, Nova Scotia, in Canada. I didn't know a soul in Canada. My only reference was the Office of Immigration and Settlement in the Union Station in Toronto; there I was to discover where I'd be working.

The farm was not very far from Toronto and so, after a short train ride, I was warmly welcomed by my new boss, Lorne Wideman. And wow, what a welcome! He and his family treated me more and more like a son than a hired hand. When they were invited out by their family or friends, I was invited too. Before meals they said grace, and in the evenings there was the reading of Scripture. Both surprised me; I'd never encountered such folk! On my first Sunday they invited me to attend church. Having never been to a Sunday morning service in my life, I wasn't anxious to go. However, since they were so kind to me I didn't wish to be impolite; I consented. The singing was good, but after the reading of the Scriptures everyone knelt for prayer. Boy, that really irritated me! I declared there and then that I would never attend church again. Oh, they kept asking me; even their two small adopted daughters couldn't understand why I wouldn't go, since they enjoyed church so much. The more they asked, the more stubborn I became. Finally, I asked Lorne not to invite me again.

Eager to explore the surrounding area, I purchased a motorcycle, but, not being used to it, I had an accident, skidding across the wet pavement and hitting my head. The next thing I remember was being asked by a doctor where I lived and worked. Barely conscious and very confused, I gave them my German address. Naturally, they weren't able to locate anyone. Eventually I was with it enough to tell them for whom I worked. Lorne fetched me and transferred me to the hospital in Toronto, where they attended to my fractured collarbone, treated my concussion and bound up my cuts and bruises. During my ten days' hospitalisation a pastor visited

me, asking if he could pray for me. I told him it would be OK, but that I doubted it would do much good for I didn't have any faith.

Even though I was laid up and no use on the farm, I never heard Lorne complain or seem angry. Bored, I began reading whatever was handy, most of it was their Christian literature. One little booklet stated that Christians owed their allegiance to Christ and that, in case of war, a Christian should register as a conscientious objector, thus avoiding taking another man's life. This made good sense for, had the established churches in Germany taken a clear stand on peace issues, maybe the war would have been prevented and millions of lives spared. Yet still I refused to go to church.

It was the autumn of 1951; the time for special revival and evangelistic meetings at the church. Unknown to me, Lorne planned how he could get me to go to the meetings. Maybe, Lorne thought, if Marion (his wife) asked her parents to invite me first to a meal, then I'd afterwards attend church with them.

'Surely, Carl, one church service won't be too hard to endure,' Marion said.

Out of politeness to my employer's wife, I went along and that evening I heard the gospel preached in a simple, straightforward way that I could understand; it sounded right and good. Obviously, the kindness of those dear folk for whom I'd come to work was paying off! That same evening I remarked how it had been great to be in church. 'I'd sure like to go again, please.'

The third evening a 'Billy Graham' type of an appeal was given and, guess what, I responded, coming to believe in the Lord Jesus Christ who'd given his life on a cross for me!

As far as the Bible was concerned, I was completely ignorant, so Marion's parents suggested I attend Ontario Bible School in a place named Kitchener. I laughed off the very idea, but in January 1952 I enrolled in a three month

course. Oh, and there was also another student — a beautiful young woman named Leota.

Leota and I completed the short course, enjoying every moment — godly teachers and other Christian students made the course an unforgettable experience.

We were married in the October of the same year, but she, a farm girl, returned to her parents' smallholding in Ohio and, to help out financially, I went back to Lorne's farm. I'd hoped to have a farm of our very own, but my low wage wouldn't stretch to such a dream.

One of the members of Lorne's church had taken me to the missionary convention of the People's Church in Toronto which, under the leadership of its pastor, Oswald J. Smith, supported missionary work in a number of countries. That planted in me the interest of missionary work. But this would mean having to go back to college, and school work had never been my strong point. And how would I be able to raise the finance? Would my English be good enough to follow the teaching, to do the necessary written work? I wrestled with such questions until the day came when the Lord seemed to say: Go ahead! With the encouragement of Leota, I enrolled in a pre-theological course at a place called Waterloo Bible College. From hauling manure and working in the fields, I needed to absorb so much more in the way of theology ... and then there was the New Testament Greek! However, when the Lord leads He also enables! Praise His name! But I wasn't facing these tasks alone – from now on Leota and I faced the challenges of life together. (All through our married life Leota has faithfully stood by my side, supporting me and being a mother to our seven children, six of which grew up and now have families of their own.) From now on it will be our story, because Leota has contributed immeasurably to our life together.

The Lord led then to two more years of college in Virginia. They were lean, hard years. At one time we didn't

have enough to pay our electric bill, but they agreed to accept some postage stamps for payment! Another time Ruby, our oldest daughter, pulled down a kettle full of boiling water, severely scalding one third of her body. The medical bills would have taken all my funds set aside for college. Through Christian friends the Lord supplied the exact amount. Leota took in washing and typing from the students. I worked first in a supermarket; then I fed chickens. I graduated in May of 1955 without any college debts! I also had a dear wife, two children and a third on the way.

Again the question arose: 'Lord, what would You have us do now?' He led us to Somalia in East Africa. There we were to be teachers-cum-evangelists in a small village in the interior. Our assignment was to begin an elementary school, but how could we approach the people, for they were highly suspicious of us.

The Lord opened up the way, but not in the way we'd expected! In the early hours we were woken up by a knocking on our door. As I opened, three men stood there; one held a spear, two had clubs. They asked for the midwife. I told them there wasn't one. They replied that Leota was a midwife. They wanted her to go with them – there was a woman in the village who'd been in labour all night. Despite my protestations, they were insistent. After a prayer, Leota decided to go with them, grabbing what she'd seen a doctor use in home deliveries. With some misgivings I saw her disappear into the dark of the night with three strangers. (I was unable to accompany her because we had our three little children with us, ages two, one, and eight weeks, who were peacefully sleeping, quite unaware what their mother was undertaking.) Nervously I watched the day dawn, looking toward the village, eager to get the first glimpse of Leota returning. Sure enough, after what seemed a lifetime, she came, accompanied by two girls, one carrying a chicken and the other a basket of eggs, because of the result of the birth of

a healthy baby boy! This brought instant acceptance by the locals. God used that birth to overcome the suspicion and the cultural distance which existed between us and the Africans. Looking back, we cannot but acknowledge the hand of God.

After being in Somalia for almost two years, with a furlough in the middle of it, our children were growing up (four of them had been born in Somalia) and we were again faced with the question: Lord, what would You have us do? The educational work which we started was to be upgraded, for which we were not qualified. Our children, those of school age, had to go to a boarding school over a thousand miles away. We considered our family life was suffering under this arrangement. So we returned home. Here too we saw the hand of God, for it was not very long until all missionaries were forced to leave the country – the school and medical facilities were taken over by the government.

Back in Ohio, we enrolled our children in school. The principal of the school asked from where we came, and what had been my work. When he heard I was a teacher he offered me a post! For the next twenty years I taught maths in that local school until my retirement in 1988

Meanwhile, we were able to have Leota's father's farm. It is a small farm in the hills of Ohio, something more for the heart than for the pocket. I am also pastoring in Turkey Run Mennonite Church, enjoying the ministry the Lord has given me. Truly He has enabled us in the small and the large tasks, to walk the paths along which He has led. To Him belongs all the praise and all the glory! Looking back, it would have been humanly impossible for us to plan all this and make it come out right. What a mighty and loving God we serve!

In the morning I got up very early to a day which promised splendour. I peered out of our bedroom window. A pink dawn was spilling across the sky. I dressed quickly and prayed for the day ahead, that God would be glorified, that the

congregation would only see and hear Him instead of us, His channels.

After the morning service, just before having Sunday lunch with the Wesselhoefts' daughter and son-in-law, Ruth and Mike Bender, their daughter Ruby Wesselhoeft, knowing that I was a midwife, whisked me off in her truck to a remote homestead where a couple, she in her mid thirties and he obviously many years older, were expecting their first child.

As she drove up to a clearing in the woods, it seemed we were outside a wooden shack joined on to a crummy blacksmith's smithy. A couple of large black mongrels barked, making me jump. One bared his teeth.

'Take no notice of them — just walk straight through,' Ruby instructed.

'This is it?' I asked.

'Yep. The husband, who sees himself as a blacksmith, built it himself. Pretty bad, eh? Just wait till you see the inside!' Ruby chuckled. 'It's overrun with stray cats and even more nasty dogs. I feel real sorry for any kid being brought up in this mess.'

The husband, a well-built, bearded man desired to live in the basic style of the Amish, but he had long discovered he couldn't join them, for he'd been married before; they do not welcome divorcees into their community. Both Mennonites and Amish recognise that marriage is for life; divorce and remarriage are simply not considered, because their life and future are built upon and around the family. (Amish are also very clean folk!)

Before being with this present wife he lived rough, drinking heavily and eating anything he could find — mostly wild dogs or ground hogs. Now it was he who felt that, if he couldn't actually be Amish, he and his wife should at least live like them. He claimed that, if the Amish women could have home births, then his wife could too. This really was

nonsense, for the Amish don't oppose modern medicine. There is nothing in their religion which prevents them from going to a doctor, taking pills or medicines, and entering the hospital when necessary. He wanted his wife to use a so-called local midwife who wasn't a midwife at all. This untrained quack tended to deliver those women who were without any medical insurance. She restricted her work to Amish or Mennonites because she knew that if anything went wrong she would not be prosecuted, for those folk don't take people to court.

'Do you really want your wife to deliver her first baby here? It's not exactly hygienic with all these cats and dogs roaming over the place, is it?' started my outspoken companion.

Looking around, it was true, for one would see better places in the third world ... and this was America!

'She really does need to go to the hospital and be delivered; I was 38 when I had Matthew and I couldn't have considered anything but a hospital delivery,' I told him, shooing away one of the many cats from getting on my lap. 'Any woman of her age about to deliver a first baby, well, in my professional opinion, she requires the expert care only hospitals can give. Imagine if anything went wrong, and with all those cats around — they are a danger to her and the unborn baby's health.'

He sat down at the homemade table and stared out of the window.

Turning to the woman, I asked her about her antenatal care. Before she could answer, he leaned across the table informing me she hadn't had any.

I looked aghast. 'None! You're in your middle thirties, expecting your first baby and you've received no professional

care? No scans? Nothing?'

She shook her head to all my questions.

'How many weeks are you?'

She shrugged. 'Thirty-nine, I think. I'm really not quite sure.'

'May I examine you?'

She and I went upstairs and she lay on a grubby bed. As I palpated her abdomen, I advised her to stop playing at being Amish and get herself admitted to the nearest hospital. She nodded in agreement.

Ruby bundled her up, ignoring the husband's protests and drove her to the hospital at Logan.

On examination, the obstetrician discovered her to have serious complications; immediately she was transferred to the large teaching hospital in Columbus, even though she possessed no medical insurance. That night she had a Caesarean section, being delivered of a small but healthy baby girl, whom she named Sarah.

16

The One Room School

I wasn't feeling my best. I'd woken up like it; I didn't know why or what was wrong.

'Maybe you're overtired,' suggested Eric. 'After all, in recent weeks we've travelled a lot of miles and led many meetings.'

I shrugged. This was the beginning of a new day which I'd intended to be a quiet one — one to be unobtrusive. It wasn't starting in the way I'd wished, but there, I needed to have sufficient faith to believe it was all for the best, for I could rest up and prepare for the next. Even so, I felt it was all a hard struggle, as if all the resources of hell were against me, for I couldn't even seem to think straight. Yet wasn't it supposed to be a glorious thing to be able to feel we are fighting in the Great Cause? So, Eric and I prayed together, more than perhaps we'd done in the past, for I couldn't help believing our ministry in the USA was on the threshold of greater things for our God — we needed to be worthy of the trust invested in us, as this was no holiday.

The next morning when 1 woke up it was with new pressures; for now my mouth hurt. Peering into the bathroom mirror and pulling down my bottom lip, I saw a cluster of

large ulcers. Feeling rotten and padding barefoot into the kitchen where Eric was pouring out a bowl of cornflakes, I pulled down my lower lip. 'Look at my mouth!' I exclaimed. 'How shall I eat solid food? Sloppy stuff or liquids might be all right, but we are dining with the Gingerichs this evening. What shall I do? I can't arrive only to tell the wife I can't manage her cooking.'

'Perhaps we'll have to buy you a few tins of Heinz baby food on the way!' Eric joked.

'Oh, you're a great help, I don't think,' I retorted with a frown. 'You wouldn't find it so funny if you felt as grotty as this. I have to speak tonight, and for quite a while ...'

I gave Matthew a look as if to say, 'And don't you joke either,' and padded back a trifle wildly, half forgetting we were engaged in a battle, for '*we wrestle not against flesh and blood, but against the world rulers of this present darkness, against the spiritual hosts of wickedness in the heavenly places*' (Ephesians 6:12). Oh, how far we Christians can wander from plain living and high thinking.

Realising I was in no mood for jokes, Eric followed me. 'Are you going to be sick? You look pale.'

'No.'

He phoned Mrs Grace Gingerich, to tell her I wouldn't be able to cope with anything but soft, easy-going food as I was decidedly unwell.

'Don't worry,' she said, 'I'll strain some of my nice chicken soup. We're just looking forward to having you all with us ...'

'Thank you. By the way, Matthew won't be with us — he'll be staying with Richard and Jewel Showalter.'"

'He'll have a real good time with those folk. Jewel Showalter is good with kids.'

'He'll probably eat them out of house and home!'

'Have a nice day. See you later here in Hartville.'

On our journey up to Hartville, Northern Ohio, we called in at a chemist where a pharmacist sold me some bright yellowish ointment which she claimed would anaesthetise the soreness long enough to let me eat and speak properly.

Arriving in Hartville way too early to call in on the Gingerichs, we decided to use our time to find Bethany Mennonite Church where we were to minister that evening.

'What a large building! Pass me the camera, Sarah, please. I really want to photograph this place.'

'I thought you'd photographed all the places we'd been to,' I said, grappling for the camera.

Over the road, on the other side of a fence, we were being watched by a single real attraction — a wide-eyed raccoon which made me smile for the first time that day. My venomous, mean spirit was being blown away like the breeze that was getting up. I like animals — I just had to try a little harder that day to be charming to Eric.

Later, as our hired car pulled into the Gingerichs' drive, brother John Gingerich, a shortish man, rushed out of his front door to greet us, urging us to 'come on in, come on in!'

His wife, who was taller and more slender, probably in her late fifties, was busy cooking in the kitchen, yet she immediately stopped what she was doing, wiped her hands on her apron, and hugged us both.

'How's your sore mouth?' she asked with obvious sensitivity.

Thanks to the pharmacist's potion, the inside of my bottom lip felt numb — it had that lack of sensation one experiences after a visit to the dentist; I certainly didn't feel as unwell as when I'd first woken up.

Flatly refusing any help, Grace ushered me into their living room where Eric was listening to John recounting his time in post war Germany where he'd worked among displaced people — those homeless because of World War II. His fascinating tale was suddenly interrupted by a sharp

rapping on the front door.

'Ah! That'll be our other guest,' John said, 'you'll enjoy meeting this young man ...'

We already knew him. It was Conrad! Only the previous year Conrad was on the YES team[1] in Wales with a young Rhoda Showalter[2] and Heidi Hochstedler.

'Hey, it's sure good to see you folks again!' exclaimed the tall, fair haired fellow, and he began to tell us how he was planning to train to become a pastor.

John's enthusiasm for our testimonies and the Passover demonstration, followed by a communion service, had a knock-on effect with his congregation, who seemed to hang on our every word. This was a church which was as disciplined for the pastor as for the members, but there was no heavy shepherding. It had recaptured the whole glorious conception of the Christian life; the congregation felt there was no honour which could be conferred upon them as great as their church membership. The pastor felt there was nothing in life to be compared with the preaching of the glorious and incomparable gospel. Encouraged, we left the church, thanking God for the place.

Once back at the Gingerichs' home, John asked me to stay on and speak the next day at the assembly in Hartville Christian School, where he was acting headmaster.

Hartville School was a Mennonite private school where a high standard of education was maintained. This was a one-roomed school. Mennonite parents want their children to learn the basics such as reading, writing, and arithmetic.

There are two distinct traditions concerning education among the various Amish and Mennonite groups in North America. The majority favour the higher education as a good and helpful experience for young people. The minority

---

1 Youth Evangelistic Service

2 Rhoda Showalter is the daughter of Richard and Jewel Showalter.

question whether high school and college lead to greater wisdom and Christian obedience. So when they were offered the local one-roomed school with a minimum of worldly influences, parents cooperated with the system. Work is for each pupil both educational and enjoyable.

I asked John what he wanted me to say.

'Just give them your testimony, as you did to the church last night,' he said, nonchalantly. 'Nothing could be easier for you.'

'But, John, how old are they? Will they understand what I'm talking about?'

Calmly, he explained how their ages ranged from about six to sixteen years. That was some age gap! To reach up to the level of a sixteen year old was surely to leave a little six year old without much comprehension; yet John didn't see a problem.

That night I settled down to get some sleep. I slept fitfully, that dissatisfying, semi-conscious sleep in which one incorporates into one's dreams the things going on around one, or there's the imagination they stimulate. I woke myself up with a start, thinking I had fallen, plunging for miles. I glanced around me and stared down at my watch. It had only just passed midnight. Hours to go before encountering those children, I thought, feeling apprehensive.

After about twenty minutes, the younger children left the school assembly hall and were filed off with their teachers where their lessons commenced. The older groups remained. Brother John Gingerich told me lessons for the seniors could be cancelled; he urged me to continue talking to them, encouraging those young Christians to ask me questions.

When I mentioned in my testimony how my parents disowned me after my baptism in water, one teenager asked me if it compared with the "ban". The "ban" is the practice of excommunication used as a means of keeping the Amish church pure. The "ban", based on 1 Corinthians 5:11, takes

many forms, from members being refused communion to having other members not eat with them, visit, or do business with them — one of the issues over which the Amish and Mennonites split in 1693. The practice of shunning is designed to bring a member back into fellowship.

I informed them how my parents had eventually welcomed me back, yet my relationship was still somewhat frosty with my mother, which was probably just a clash of personalities between her and myself.

Question after question came to me and what I'd started at 8:30 A.M. hadn't finished at 11 A.M. Some assembly!

The seniors were eventually filed outside on the lawn for Eric to photograph them with John and me. The girls all looked so attractive, dressed, not unlike the Amish with cape dresses; the cape is an additional piece of material that sits over the waist of a dress, designed for feminine modesty. As we sat around on the lawn, they asked me why I kept my hair short and could they touch and feel it. Another asked if I always wore skirts below my knees, and where did I buy my cardigan? One whispered in my ear how she wished she could be allowed to be more "with it" and buy her clothes from one of the large London department stores instead of wearing the traditional dress.

Another sixteen year old asked me about our Royal Family, and what did I feel about three out of the Queen's four children having failed marriages. 'Your future king, Prince Charles, committed adultery with that Mrs Parker-Bowles, didn't he?'

I nodded. 'Maybe he'll repent,' I said.

'How do you feel about divorce?' she continued.

I knew that marriage is sacred to both Mennonites and Amish. For them, and for Eric and me, it's a total commitment and for life. Divorce and remarriage for the Mennonites and Amish are not considered, and she wanted to know if I felt the same.

Worldwide Christian teaching claims that marriage was ordained by God for companionship between one man and one woman, for monogamy was the Divine order from the beginning. Adam had one wife and this seems to have been the early rule. The Old Testament tells of men of faith who took second wives, yet, in every case it also tells of the trouble this brought on them. The Church reinstated the original rule as an absolute necessity for elders (see: 1 Timothy 3:2; Titus 1:6) and as an example for all Christians. Marriage should be a lifelong partnership built on love. *"Husbands, love your wives as Christ loved the church and gave himself up for her"* (Ephesians 5:25). The physical union created *'one flesh'* (Ephesians 5:31) — *'For this reason a man shall leave his father and mother and be joined to his wife and the two shall become one flesh'.* Clearly, monogamy is the Divine order set out here, producing a mutual dependence and requiring that both partners must respect the wishes of the other — *"Be subject to one another"* (Ephesians 5:21). Christian teaching condemns every relationship and action which damages the family, including adultery (Exodus 20:14), infidelity (Malachi 2:14), fornication (1 Corinthians 6:12-20), lust (Matthew 5:28), homosexual practices (Leviticus 18:22), and incest (Leviticus 18:6). Christian teaching doesn't allow divorce, except for the innocent party where there's been adultery — *'Whoever divorces his wife, except for unchastity, and marries another, commits adultery; and he who marries a divorced woman commits adultery'* (Matthew 19:9). It is on the basis of this exception that some Christian churches allow the remarriage of the innocent party. However, it is clear from Christ's words that this is the only exception, though some denominations don't even allow this. Nevertheless, I've known those who divorce for other reasons, such as either extreme cruelty or other unreasonable types of unsocial behaviour and then, later, remarry. They alone stand before

our God; I don't feel I can stand in any sort of judgement. *'If thou, 0 Lord shouldst mark iniquity, Lord, who could stand?'* (Psalm 130:3)

Sadly, it was soon time to say our goodbyes, and they all waved and waved until they could no longer be seen.

During the journey back to our apartment at Rosedale we stopped at a McDonalds. Swallowing a mouthful of hamburger, Eric asked what John had written in a journal of mine. I told him he'd written:

> *What a blessing you have been to Grace and me,*
> *the Bethany Mennonite Church and the Hartville*
> *Christian School!*
> *It's a blessing to know Jesus as Savior and Lord ...*
> *may the Father bless you!*
>
> *John and Grace Gingerich*
> *Hartvil!e, Ohio.*

'I'm really touched, but I feel they were more of a blessing to us; don't you agree?' I said.

Eric nodded. 'Oh, and by the way, how's your mouth now ... any better, love?' he asked.

'Yes. That ointment has really helped ... well done, the pharmacologist. Better still, thanks to God for the prayers of His people ... and for the Lord who never fails!'

'Amen to that!' exclaimed Eric.

When it was time for us to leave the States (I didn't want the trip to be over) there was William at the Columbus airport waving us goodbye.

'I'll pray for you, William. I'll write.'

He smiled. 'Yes please ... keep in touch.'

17

Pennsylvanian Dutch Recipes

Farm appetites are big and so are farm meals, especially in the Pennsylvanian Dutch country. Breakfast usually includes ham, eggs, potatoes and even pie! Lunchtime is traditionally called dinnertime. Supper is around 5:30 P..M. The really festive Pennsylvanian Dutch meal normally includes seven sweets and seven savouries!

If you are not interested in cooking, please skip this chapter — it's all recipes.

There is much of the German influence in Pennsylvanian Dutch cooking, and sauerkraut and dumplings are as popular in Homes County and Lancaster County as in Bavaria. But a Shoofly pie is pure Pennsylvanian Dutch.

Meat Loaf
(Beef can replace the ham and pork)
12oz (340g) minced ham
12oz (340g) minced pork
3oz (85g) fine breadcrumbs

7oz (200ml) milk
2 eggs
4 tbsp minced onion
½ stick celery, finely chopped
¼ tsp mustard powder
⅛ tsp pepper

Combine all ingredients and mix thoroughly. Shape into a loaf and place into a baking tin or shallow ovenproof dish. Bake in a very moderate oven (325°F, 170°C, Gas Mark 3) for 1½ hours. Serve hot or cold. It's nice with tomato sauce and tossed salad.

We had this in the Dutch Kitchen Amish Restaurant in Plain City, and also at the home of Irene and Emery Helmuth, who were a host and maintenance couple at the Rosedale Mennonite Missions, Irwin, Ohio.

Banana Bread
(can be purchased in Amish shops, e.g. in Plain City, OH)

4oz (114g) butter or margarine
7oz (200g) sugar
2 eggs
8oz (227g) mashed ripe bananas (3 small)
6oz (170g) plain flour
2oz (57g) oatmeal
1 tsp baking powder
½ tsp bicarbonate of soda
½ tsp salt
2oz (57g) chopped nuts

Cream butter and sugar and beat in the eggs one at a time. Stir in mashed bananas. Combine with oatmeal, baking powder, bicarbonate of soda and salt. Beat into first mixture. Stir in nuts. Pour mixture into a greased loaf tin and bake in a moderate oven (350°F, 180°C, Gas Mark 4) for 65 minutes. Cool overnight before slicing.

Shoofly Pie

Shortcrust pastry for single-crust pie
5oz (140ml) treacle
5oz (140ml) boiling water
¾ tsp. bicarbonate of soda
6oz (170g) plain flour
3oz (85g) granulated sugar
4oz (113g) brown sugar
1 tsp. baking powder
2 tbsp. cooking fat

Prepare pastry and line 9-inch (23cm) pie plate. Combine treacle and boiling water and mix well. Stir in soda. Cool. Mix flour, sugars and baking powder and rub in fat until crumbly. Spread half of crumbs in pastry and put half of treacle mixture over. Repeat. Bake in hot oven (425°F, 220°C, Gas Mark 7) for 10 minutes. Reduce heat (325°F, 170°C, Gas Mark 3) and bake until set (25-35 minutes).

Barbecued Beef Sandwiches

4oz (113g) cooked roast beef
4 tbsp. ketchup
1 tbsp. vinegar
2 tsp. brown sugar
¼ tsp. pepper
1 tbsp. water
2 hamburger buns, split and toasted

Cut beef into small thin pieces. Mix ketchup, vinegar, brown sugar, pepper and water and bring to the boil. Add beef and simmer for 5 minutes, stirring frequently. Serve hot between halves of buns. Two sandwiches.

A pretty young Mennonite teenager served me with this in our first trip to the Dutch Kitchen. It looked awful to me, and tasted even worse. Eric, who I teased was a dustbin in a previous life, tasted my BBQ beef sandwich and finished it off!

Pecan Pie

Shortcrust pastry for single crust pie
4 tbsp. butter
6oz (170g) brown sugar
Pinch of salt
6½ oz (190ml) dark corn syrup
3 eggs, beaten
1 tsp. vanilla essence
4oz (113g) pecan or walnut halves

Prepare pastry and line 9-inch (23 cm) pie plate. Cream butter with sugar and salt. Stir in syrup, beaten eggs and vanilla. Spread nuts evenly on pastry and pour mixture over them. Bake in a hot oven (450°F, 230°C, Gas Mark 8) 10 minutes, reduce heat (350°F, 180°C, Gas Mark 4) and bake for 30 minutes or until set.

We first sampled this at the Dutch Kitchen in Plain City. OH. Very nice if one has a sweet tooth!

Brownies

4oz (113g) butter or margarine
7oz (200g) sugar
2 eggs
1 tsp. vanilla essence
2oz (57g) unsweetened chocolate
3oz (85g) plain flour
½ tsp. baking powder
¼ tsp. salt
2oz (57g) chopped nuts
chocolate icing (optional)

Cream butter and sugar together and beat in eggs and vanilla. Melt chocolate and add to mixture. Combine flour, baking powder and salt in, blending well. Add nuts. Spread mixture in buttered 8 inch (20cm) square baking tin and bake in a moderate oven (350°F, 180°C, Gas Mark 4) for 30-35 minutes. Cool in tin and ice with chocolate icing, if desired. Cut into squares.

Blueberry muffins

7oz (200g) plain flour
2½ tsp. baking powder
¾ tsp. salt
3 tbsp. sugar
1 egg, beaten
4oz (125ml) milk
4 tbsp. cooking oil
5oz (125g) blueberries

Sieve together flour, baking powder, salt and sugar. Combine egg, milk and oil and add to flour mixture. Stir just until blended. Fold in blueberries gently and pour into greased

patty tins (two thirds full). Bake in a moderately hot oven (400'F, 200'C, Gas Mark 6) for 25 minutes.

Peanut Butter Bread

4oz (113g) peanut butter
2 tbsp. salad oil
5oz (142g) sugar
1 egg
½ pt + 2 tbsp. (290ml) milk
8oz (227g) plain flour
3 tsp. baking powder
¼ tsp. salt

Cream peanut butter, oil and sugar together. Beat in egg, add milk and mix well. Sieve flour, baking powder and salt together and stir into first mixture. Pour into buttered loaf tin and bake in a moderate oven ((350°F, 180°C, Gas Mark 4) for one hour or until inserted knife comes out clean.

It's an acquired taste! We purchased some in Plain City at the Amish shop and then gave it away to some Mennonites who loved it.

Apple Butter

4pt (2.21ltr) apple juice
8lb (3.6kg) cooking apples
2½ lb (1.1kg) sugar
3 tsp cinnamon

Peel, core and quarter apples. Place in large saucepan and pour apple juice over them. Simmer gently until very soft. Add sugar and cinnamon and stir until sugar dissolves. Continue cooking, stirring frequently, until very thick and a rich brown colour. Spoon into sterilised jars and seal.

Fudge Brownies
(For Death by Chocolate, make a double recipe)

¼ cup (55g) margarine or butter
6oz (170g) semi-sweet chocolate chips
¾ cup (170g) sugar
²⁄₃ cup (75g) flour
½ tsp. vanilla
¼ tsp. baking powder
¼ tsp. salt
2 eggs
2oz chopped nuts

1. Heat the oven to 350°F, 180°C, Gas Mark 4.
2. Grease the bottom only of a square pan (8" x 8" x 2").
3. In a large bowl melt 6oz chocolate chips and ¼ cup of margarine in the microwave, stirring until smooth (or melt together in a pan over the stove).
4. Stir in all the remaining ingredients, except the nuts, beat real hard with a wooden spoon until smooth.
5. Stir in nuts. Spread in the square pan with a rubber spatula.
6. Bake until the centre is set, about 30 minutes. Let brownies cool completely.

Death by Chocolate

9"x 3" pan of brownies
2 packages of chocolate mousse prepared
2 cups whipped cream (or more)
8 health bars, crushed (English toffee crushed
    with chocolate)
1 cup chopped pecans

1. Prepare brownies, cool, crumble and place half of crumbs
   in a large glass bowl.
2. Prepare chocolate mousse according to directions and
   spread half of mousse over crumbled brownies. Sprinkle
   with half of pecans. Repeat all layers beginning again with
   crumbled brownies.
3. Refrigerate for several hours or overnight. Serve.

18

Wading Through Treacle?

A little while after we had settled back in our home, we heard from Jewel how William had started to attend the Mennonite church in Mechanicsburg, but that he hadn't made a firm commitment. We continued to pray.

Then, joy of joys, the following Christmas, a letter dropped through our door from Irene Helmuth, another of our Rosedale friends. She told me that William had accepted the Lord Jesus Christ as his own personal Saviour; not only had he confessed with his lips, but that he'd witnessed by going through the waters of baptism. Our God is still on the throne!

''In the same way, I tell you, there is rejoicing in the presence of the angels of God over one sinner who repents.' (Luke 15:10)

In the year 2001 I acquired a Nurse/Manager's post in Colwyn Bay. My husband asked me to seat myself in my office at my new desk so he could photograph me; he was 'humbly proud' I had the job! However, when I saw the colour prints I was quite disappointed. I had blinked due to the flash.

'I've blinked in all three of the photographs,' I

150

complained. 'In fact, I looked half asleep!'

He said nothing.

The next morning I was getting ready for work and noticed how my eyelids were, in fact, drooping. I tried hard to open my eyes wide, but the lids kept drooping.

Must be sheer tiredness, I thought, and then made off to work.

Lis, my deputy, and I wanted to get to know one another. With mounds of ever-growing paperwork, telephones ringing and various interruptions it was difficult.

'Look, Lis, why don't we meet up at the new restaurant in Craig-y-Don and enjoy a meal together?'

She agreed and we met up on the following Monday at 12:30 P.M.

Lis watched me slowly picking over the main course. 'Do I have a bigger mouth than you, Sarah?' she chuckled. 'Goodness me ... I've finished my chicken and you're still picking, still eating ...'

I apologised. 'Sorry, but if I try and talk to you and eat too, well, I'll choke.'

One week or so later a local GP visited one of his patients. Lis wasn't available to accompany him, so I left my desk to chaperone the patient.

'We'll go in the lift,' I told him, but the lift was already in use and stuck on the top floor.

After examining his patient the GP and I made our way back down the main staircase, me being steadied by the handrail.

'You seem slow today, Sarah,' he remarked. 'Are you okay?'

I told him I was just fine, but I overheard a visitor saying: 'Makes you wonder who are the staff and who are the patients.'

I pretended I hadn't heard her cutting remark, yet I knew I was bone tired — but then I worked hard.

'You work too hard and such long hours,' Eric reassured me. 'It's not surprising you get tired ... also it must be stressful to start this new job. It's a pity we didn't have a holiday before you took up the post.'

In 2003 we decided to fly out to Malta for two weeks, combining a relaxing holiday with Sister Helen Curmi's seventieth birthday. She was living in a convent in St Julians with three other nuns.

One of the youngest nuns was cooking the 'birthday meal'. We were invited. As we sat at the table I ate the delicious food, yet I noticed that everyone had finished yonks before me; I also coughed and choked somewhat when anyone distracted me.

Worried I would spoil the birthday meal I apologised for being so slow. The nun who'd cooked the meal presumed she'd overfed me with the amount she'd served me and swiftly took away the food left on my plate.

'It was just too much ... too much for you, wasn't it?' Helen remarked, trying to be kind.

A day or so later Eric and I visited Sister Josephine in Rabat. We'd had a problem finding the Convent of the Sacred Heart in Tal Virtu Road. Our taxi driver didn't know Rabat well and left us in the wrong part of the Maltese town. Eric and I walked this way and that and it was quite some time before we located the convent where a worried Sister Josephine was waiting for us.

'We got lost,' I explained, feeling tired ... very tired indeed. My legs ached so that I felt as if I'd been walking through treacle.

Once more, we were treated to a delicious luncheon. We were able to help ourselves from the dishes; I helped myself to a small amount, remembering Helen's birthday meal through which I struggled.

Josephine stared at my plate and asked me, 'Is that all you want? It won't even keep a bird alive!'

After the meal Josephine showed us around. Realising how tired I looked, she took us in the lift to see the newly refurbished little chapel before allowing us to relax in a lounge. Another nun, also named Josephine, offered to drive us part way to our hotel, explaining how we could get a bus for the remainder of the journey. We thanked her, but I was much too weary to go along with her plans; we phoned again for a taxi.

We were staying at the beautiful Topaz Hotel. On our final day we made our way to the airport where we were told our plane would be delayed.

'I'm off to the loo,' I told my husband. 'I shall not be long.'

Coming out of the loo I stood and stared over at the wash basin, which seemed so far from my reach. I wondered how I was going to walk to it without falling over, for I couldn't seem to keep my balance. Another woman was already drying her hands. I called across to her, asking for help, but she just eyed me up and down, tutted loudly and walked out.

Somehow I made it, but how was I going to make my way across Malta's airport lounge, to where Eric was seated? Another woman was about to leave the 'rest room' so I asked her to help me. Believing I was either drunk or drugged, she started to refuse me, but I quickly explained that I was not inebriated; she helped and I was again seated next to my husband.

'Don't let go of me,' I said. 'I'm frightened of falling over. I just don't know what's the matter.'

During the in-flight meal I had a problem swallowing, so much of my food was again consumed by Eric.

'When we get back home you really must go and see our doctor, Sarah.'

I nodded.

About ten days later I was busy dictating some work when I began to feel more than dog tired — too weary to

continue. I wanted to cry.

Eric drove me to Glan Clwyd Hospital where I saw a doctor who said she could remember seeing someone like me in a textbook when she was a student.

'Have you heard of Myasthenia Gravis?' she questioned.

'I think so. I don't know anything about it, though.'

'Well, it's about as rare as hens' teeth,' she began. 'You'll have doctors, students and everyone coming to look at you, because they probably won't ever see another case. You'll be like a celebrity.'

She admitted me to a women's medical ward where a young nurse placed a 'nil by mouth' sign over my bed, for she believed I had a rare choking disease! I was so hungry, but she flatly refused to allow me anything to eat.

After taking my medical 'history', writing down everything about my condition, a Medical Registrar fetched another colleague.

'We're going to do a Tensilon Test. If you do have Myasthenia Gravis then the test will show positive. It was indeed positive. The Registrar started me on a very low dose of Prednisolone (a steroid) and a large dose of Mestinon which caused me serious problems with my pulse, making it too slow, causing me to worsen.

I was eventually discharged from that hospital. I was told I would soon get to see a Consultant Neurologist, but it could take months and months before I would eventually see one.

Months, I thought, why months? Surely I'd be okay by then — surely it would be all cleared up by the time I got to see a Neurologist. I was wrong! Once I was home my son checked it out on the Internet. He asked how to spell the disease. I didn't know. Finally he discovered it was MYASTHENIA GRAVIS. He found a so-called "expert" in Venezuela.

However, this Consultant in Venezuela recommended treatment which not only cost a lot, but it drastically

weakened me, causing me to go into myasthenia crisis. Finally, I saw a Dr Richard White at HMS Stanley Hospital in North Wales, under whose care I became stabilised. It became his decision, though, to pass me over to the eminent Dr Hart at the Walton Hospital, Liverpool, where I realised I would have this M.G. forever.

My confrontations with bodily illnesses have caused me to think hard concerning Divine healing, its relationship to the medical profession of which I was once a part, and the times when miracles just don't happen, causing the patient to remain unhealed.

When I was diagnosed as a Myasthenic, I was rapidly surrounded by a number of caring friends. They strongly believe in God — a great and wonderful God who is very much alive — a God who is able to do exceedingly abundantly above all that we can ask or even think. (Ephesians 3:20). On both sides of the Atlantic, in the little Mediterranean island of Malta, and in the immediate locality, God's people prayed earnestly for me. One of my dearest friends has even taken communion on a daily basis for me.

Among my Christian friends are those who home in on Isaiah 53:5 '... *with His stripes we are healed'.* They believe it is an unconditional promise to His people, to give healing to those who believe and fulfil these conditions.

Just before the Christmas of 2003, an ex-work colleague telephoned me, asking me how I was.

'No better,' I replied. 'I'm just exactly the same as ever.'

'I think you must have had this Myasthenia Gravis kicking in for quite a while. You see, I noticed —,' Marion said.

'What?' I asked her, 'What had you noticed?'

Marion explained how tired I'd looked, how slow I'd been on the stairs. 'And then there were your eyes. They were like slits when you tried to look up,' she continued. 'You looked a bit Oriental!'

' 'I worked long hours,' I answered, brushing aside her other remarks, clenching my teeth.

My eyes were wet when she left the phone. Then she recalled the number, saying she needed to share something with me.

'All right. What is it?' I asked, wanting really to hiss at the phone.

She explained how her brother-in-law, over in South Africa, having read James 5, had been miraculously healed from a serious heart condition.

'If you read that, and call upon the elders ... oh, you can be healed too, Sarah.'

I agreed, eventually replacing the receiver in its cradle.

Acting on James 5:14 –15: *'Is anyone of you sick? He should call the elders of the church to pray over him and anoint him with oil in the Name of the Lord. And the prayer offered in faith will make the sick person well; the Lord will raise him up. If he has sinned he will be forgiven,'* the Pastor and one of the members of the congregation visited me. I was anointed and they prayed for me ... some of the time they prayed in tongues. So far, nothing has changed; I am just as I was.

However, from my knowledge of God's Word and the experience of other believers, it would appear that the Lord doesn't always intervene in the way we would like.

'Trophimus I left at Miletus sick' (2 Tim 4:20).

'Three times I besought the Lord about this, that it should leave me; but He said, "My grace is sufficient for you ..." ' (2 Cor. 12: 7-10).

I find the argument that Paul's thorn in the flesh wasn't a medical condition very unconvincing.

Looking at my illness in another light ... in a more positive way, there are certain things I *can* do. My beloved friend Alice, in Ireland, reminded me softly, 'You can pray.'

'I know that,' I replied.

And then our son Matthew said without a tone of surprise in his deep voice, 'You know, Mum, there are lots of things you can do. After all, you spent all those years, when you were young, as an artist. You said you'd take it up again. And there's no Dorothy around to stop you. So get on with it!'

When Matthew returned home after spending three months in America, he found my sketchbook almost three-quarters full.
' 'Wow, Mum, these drawings are ...' he gasped, a hand gripping his throat, 'these are amazing! So, what with that and now with your writing — make use of them.'

Unsmiling, I said, 'I hate having this awful Myasthenia Gravis, but there are mornings when I wake up and look forward to the day.'

Yet I loathe the days when I am judged: 'Oh you don't have enough faith.' Should I really allow myself to be judged by those 'well-meaning folk', or should I look to our loving Heavenly Father who is Sovereign, who could heal me with the blink of an eye, or He can choose to make me wait until that wonderful day when I shall be given a new body like His glorious body?

The late Leith Samuel once reminded me: 'Let God be God.'

19

Letter to Lydia

At home
22nd August, 2007

Dearest Lydia,

Peering at my calendar I realised it is today forty-five years since I came to know the Lord Jesus Christ as my Saviour. I'd prefer to say that I also came on that day to know Him as my LORD. However, that would not be totally honest. To know Him as my LORD has become, and indeed is, a daily offering. I've wanted Him to treat me like a lump of clay ... amazing in the hands of the potter, to be formed into a magnificent pot! Even so, the process can be quite painful, can't it? He certainly hasn't finished with me; there's so much still to do as yet! What a task, eh?

My old Granny had a rocking chair. She would rock and rock away, backwards and forwards, yet she was going nowhere. Since I have had this wretched illness I have felt useless ... here, yet as if going nowhere. I spoke to the Lord (yes, I really can claim Him as LORD now!) concerning my feelings. You see, Lydia, I've been aware of my other friends being so busy for the LORD. In His service they're busy in the Church and some are preparing to help overseas; and here

I am, almost a prisoner here due to this Oculopharyngeal Muscular Dystrophy. How could I be of any value? How could I serve Him?

The LORD heard my cry and, suddenly, I was burdened in my prayer life for those in prison. Now this was an enigma. I didn't know anyone in prison and I was certainly unable to become a prison visitor. So why the burden? My answer came about a couple of weeks later. Helen Curmi sent me a Christian newspaper, and on the back page was a letter from an Italian prisoner. The letter pulled at my heartstrings and I telephoned the editor of the paper, asking for his name and whereabouts.

I wrote to him, introducing myself, and about a week or so later I received a letter from him. It was all in Italian and I know no more than about six Italian words! Anxious to know the contents, I decided to pray for someone who would translate it. However, before I'd even begun to ask the LORD the answer came! How? Well, Helen telephoned me and I asked her if she knew Italian, for many Maltese people do. She didn't, but a fellow nun was fluent in the language.

'Carmen will help you,' Helen volunteered! And Carmen has been an absolute treasure. In my second letter to the Italian, this thirty-five year old who is married with two beautiful young sons (one is 9, the other just 7 years) I asked how I could help him. The reply came. He told me how ashamed he was; all he wanted was to be forgiven by God — yet he didn't know how.

I telephoned "Lifewords" (previously the Scripture Gift Mission) in London and they sent me some little booklets in Italian. To cut a long story short, he is now a born again Christian!

Another new Christian, also a prisoner, translated for him. This man had been reading my letters. Well, he had to, didn't he? In the reading of my letters and translating them, he discovered the Gospel. He too is now a believer!

The story doesn't stop there. The first Italian needed some shoes, size 11. I was owed some money, and when I received it I had not only enough for a good pair of shoes, but enough for six pairs of socks, four T-shirts, two pairs of trousers, stationery and two sets of felt tip pens for his two sons, along with some cash. I had £49 over, which just covered the postage. Isn't the Lord wonderful?

A dear friend in Ireland kept reminding me that underneath are the everlasting arms. I experienced this during the time Eric was in hospital. My beloved husband was rushed into Bangor Hospital here in North Wales. Eric was bleeding heavily, and, catheterised, he was diagnosed with prostate cancer. What a shock.

Eric has been my rock, helping me, doing for me what I couldn't do for myself; now he wasn't here. A couple of my closest friends helped me by getting some shopping and visiting Eric in hospital. However, I needed help with heaps more than that and on a regular basis. So I contacted a local social worker who arranged for someone to clean our house and to do my shopping. Wiltshire Farm Foods delivered meals every Thursday, and placed them in my deep freezer.

I was all set up and a gem of a woman arrived, all ready to clean our apartment; then she dropped a bombshell by telling me our vacuum cleaner was faulty.

'You'll need to buy a new one,' she told me. 'I can't clean without a vacuum.' I hadn't a clue how I could buy a new vacuum cleaner. Sure, I had enough money, but I didn't have the strength to physically purchase one. I was about to cry out to the Lord when I felt I should turn on the television! I wondered why. Anyway, I turned it on and across the screen I read:

HAS YOUR VACUUM CLEANER BROKEN?
WHY NOT PURCHASE A SWIVEL SWEEPER?

I telephoned the number given, paid for it via my debit card, and two days later my gem of a cleaning lady was delighted with it. So much so that she bought one for herself and one for her parents! Isn't the Lord wonderful?

Before I close this lengthy epistle I really must share with you about one more joyful answer to prayer. Alice, my friend in Ireland, kept telling me how I have a ministry in prayer, yet I don't see that. I just see that I have plenty of time . . . time to pray. Anyway, Jenny in Blackpool contacted me. She's a delightful woman who always has the knack of cheering me up, making me laugh. Jenny has a splendid sense of humour. However, on this occasion she was serious. She had phoned me to ask me to pray for a baby boy. (To protect him and his family I'll call the baby Timothy, rather than disclose his real name – OK?) Anyway, Timothy was born on the 3rd March 2007, in the South of England. Sadly, Timothy's mother was ten days over her expected date of delivery. Timothy appeared to be normal, yet he was sluggish with his feeding. Soon Sally and her husband (Ben) were worried. Timothy became stiff and jaundiced. Sally and Ben found him difficult to wake up. Sick with worry, they rushed him to the hospital. The paediatric doctor wondered if Tim had meningitis and admitted him to the intensive care unit.

Timothy was fed via an intravenous infusion and they continuously monitored him through an E.E.G. An MRI showed severe brain damage. Sally and Ben are born again Christians. Sally grew up on the mission field – her parents were missionaries in China; they are now retired and living in the west country, here in the UK. They were desperately in need of 24/7 prayer when Jenny telephoned me, asking me to pray. I did, and I wasn't alone; prayer via the Internet went around the world, crossing all Christian denominations and geographical boundaries.

Timothy was finally discharged home, and by the time he was ready for his 10 week check-up, the paediatric

consultant declared: 'Timothy is functioning like any other normal baby. He's just fine!'

Oh, and by the way, Lydia, you must be wondering about my beloved husband. Well, Eric still has his catheter, but his results are more than encouraging. The consultant urologist doesn't need to see him for another four months. How great is our God!

Now I really must bring this letter to a close.

Do keep in touch.

Blessings

Much love as ever in Him,

Sarah

20

And So Finally

Before I bring this book to an end with a story that may ring a bell, I would like to include something that Richard Showalter has written in appreciation of the contribution Eric and I made to God's work during our time in the USA:

"Sarah, Eric, and Matthew were a breath of fresh air at Rosedale, Ohio, USA, wafted by the Holy Spirit all the way from North Wales. When they came, we had little understanding of the sacrifices they made in coming or the treasure that they were bringing. But God quickly began to open our eyes.

"It was the spontaneous, unpretentious beauty of their testimony that took us by surprise — and changed us. For some, it meant meeting Jesus for the first time. For others, it meant new steps of discipleship in grace. Sarah was never predictable, always full of life and joy in Christ. Whatever the occasion of our being with her, we met not only Sarah but also Jesus.

"The surprises of God are amply illustrated in Sarah's story as she writes it, filled with the unexpected twists of irony and sudden bursts of humor that fill the lives of Spirit-

led cross-cultural witnesses. For though she probably didn't quite know how to express it to her new-found Gentile Christian friends, Sarah has always been a missionary in the tradition of the first disciples of Jesus ever since she noticed the time on that clock and knew that her heart, too — like John Wesley's — had been strangely warmed.

"Of course, her acquaintances often didn't immediately recognize her unique ministry. Like the apostle Paul, she was 'unknown, yet known'. But the longer she walked among us the more certainly we knew that this daughter of Abraham, always a bit out of place in that strange Gentile Christian world, was supremely 'in place' in Christ. She could be declared dead, jilted, ill, deceived by a trusted friend, misunderstood as an 'innocent abroad' — but she was always securely and supremely in Christ.

"No, she never became a long-term missionary in India, although still she might! But I reckon that even more than she knew, she has always been a witness to 'foreigners', first in England and then in the United States. This book, laced with the life of God, is simply one more fragrance-filled, remarkable step in bearing that witness. Thank you, Sarah, for walking among us with so much patience and wisdom — sparkling with joy in Christ all the way."

It has been good to know that my Jewish roots were of value in communicating the breadth of the foundations of our faith. As a youngster, growing up within Jewish confines, much was taken for granted, with no knowledge of being 'different'. However, as a Messianic Jewess I have been led into a greater understanding of the Christian heritage; the very source of our faith lies in the living Jewish traditions. One discovers thereby more fully what it means to be a believer, and that insolubly and eternally Christianity cannot be separated from my Jewish roots — an enrichment to be handed on.

We were very grateful to Mennonite friends, including Richard and Jewel Showalter, and especially Ruth and Mike Bender, who cared for eight-year-old Matthew when our journeys were likely to be too long and arduous. They loved him, "adopting" him as one of their fast-growing family. Ruth Bender, whom I have come to love as my sister, has written:

"The highlight of our first meeting was the Passover Seder that Sarah shared for a Sunday service at Turkey Run Mennonite Church. The rich symbolism of the Passover menu and how it is served added meaning to our familiar communion service. We celebrated together in adoration the memorial of the death and resurrection of our Savior, Jesus Christ."

Some years ago I was told the now familiar story of a young headstrong man in his early twenties, who left his godly family to go and make his fortune. He failed.

Any money he made was spent at the roulette tables in various gambling dens, on strong drink, and loose women. His lifestyle eventually collapsed around him and his hedonism turned to crime.

The time came when he, after several years, was to be released from prison. He wanted nothing more than to return to the bosom of his family. Yet, surely, they would not have him back — after all, had he not disgraced their good name by his criminal activities?

Instead of just turning up on their doorstep, he decided to write them a letter. This is what he wrote:

Dear Mum and Dad,

I know that I have been nothing but a very real disgrace to you. I'm hardly worthy to be called your son any more. On Thursday I am to be released from prison. I would very much like to come home again. However, I realise that

you may not want me. I shall be on the train, leaving the city where I was in detention; it calls in at the town where you live – once my home. If you decide to have me back please put a large white ribbon on one of the branches of the old tree just at the end of the station. If I see no ribbons I will stay on the train and travel on.

From your ever-loving son.

The young man boarded the train. When it finally pulled in at the railway station, he leaned out of the window and looked to see if there was a white ribbon in the big old tree. What he saw was virtually every branch covered with white ribbons, each tied into a large bow.

Jesus said: '... *there is rejoicing in the presence of the angels of God over one sinner who repents.'* (Luke 15:10)

He went on to tell a parable similar to the 'white ribbon' story, but this time it was about the welcome awaiting those who desire to return to God. In this parable of the prodigal son, the wayward lad became disillusioned with his lifestyle in the far country, and said, 'I will set out and go back to my father and say to him: "Father, I have sinned against heaven and against you. I am no longer worthy to be called your son".' (Luke 15:18)

There was no grudging welcome in the father's home — anything but! Luke (Chapter 15:22, 23) describes the glad reaction of the father to his son's repentance. 'Quick! Bring the best robe and put it on him. Put a ring on his finger and sandals on his feet. Bring the fattened calf and kill it. Let's have a feast and celebrate.'

All of us have to face the future; it is wonderful to do so trusting the Lord Jesus Christ rather than to be a victim of loneliness, fear and uncertainty concerning our eternal destiny.

God does not use just the spiritual giants, but He calls ordinary folk just like you and me, those who are faithfully

prepared to give themselves to Him and live for Him.

So, if having read this book, and you want to know if God, the loving heavenly Father, would accept you too, then believe He has a very special tree all covered in white ribbons, just for you.

'If you ask anything in My Name. I will do it.' (John 14:14). God has not changed since biblical times ... the Lord still reigns.

> Come, let us sing of a wonderful love,
> Tender and true;
> Out of the heart of the Father above,
> Streaming to me and to you:
> Wonderful love
> Dwells in the heart of the Father above.

(Robert Walmsley 1831 - 1905)

167

References

Information Regarding the Passover

Seder
This word means 'order of service'.

Candles
The woman of the house uses a head covering, such as a scarf, when she lights two candles, shading her eyes from their glow and saying the following blessing:

Blessed art thou, O Lord our God, King of the Universe, who has sanctified us by his commandments and has commanded us to kindle the festival lights.

Kiddush
This word is Hebrew for sanctification. Everyone present fills their wineglass before the head of the house says two standard blessings:

Blessed art thou, O Lord our God, King of the Universe, Creator of the fruit of the vine.

Blessed art thou, O Lord our God, King of the Universe, who has kept us alive and sustained us, and has enabled us to reach this season.

Everyone now drinks before reclining over the table, leaning to the left side.

The First Handwashing
The leader, or the man of the house, washes his hands, signifying his fitness to conduct the Seder.

Parsley
This first ritual is performed now, symbolising the event in the Exodus story. Everyone present takes a piece of parsley, dips it into salt water and listens to the following blessing:

Blessed art thou, O Lord our God, King of the Universe, Creator of the fruit of the earth.

Parsley reminds us of the hyssop used to daub the blood on the doorposts. (See Exodus 12:22.)

Breaking of the Middle Matzo
The leader of the Seder breaks the middle of the three matzos in two, wraps the smaller piece in a serviette and hides it. This is then known as the aphikomen. He hides this and the youngest child present is the one who'll usually have to hunt for it later. ('Aphikomen' means 'dessert' or 'that which is to come'. It is the last morsel to be eaten.)

The Forthtelling
The Exodus story is related in a series of questions, readings, prayers, and rabbinical sayings. It is usual nowadays to omit this section as it is very long!

The Second Handwashing
Everyone performs this prior to eating all the foods.

Matzos
A blessing, like our grace, is said, but one is said for the foods soon to be eaten, and the other said for the matzos.

Bitter Herbs
Another ritual takes place, again recalling the bitter slavery in Egypt.

The Sandwich
The sandwich ritual was instituted by a rabbi at the time of the Second Temple and was observed by Jesus when He gave sop to Judas.

The Meal
Only now is it permitted to eat the food prepared.

The Concealed Aphikomen
For Christians, the producing of the hidden aphikomen is one of the most significant moments.

Blessing after Food
This is a long section of grace after meals and prayers of thanksgiving. Some of it may be omitted. The third cup of wine, drunk at the end of the section, also has significance for Christians.

Hallelujah
The Seder now reaches a climax of praise through the singing of hymns and psalms.

A psalm is also sung: Psalm 126. Grace, or the blessing is then recited also after the meal.

> *Blessed art thou, O Lord our God, King of the Universe,*
> *who feeds the whole world through his goodness,*
> *with grace, loving kindness and mercy.*
> *He gives bread to all flesh, for his loving kindness is everlasting.*
> *Through his great goodness, we have never lacked,*
> *and may we never lack sustenance for ever and ever,*
> *for his great name's sake.*
> *For he feeds and maintains all, and does good to all,*
> *and prepares food for all his creatures which he has created.*
> *Blessed art thou, O Lord, who nourishes all.*

The third 'cup' of wine for us represents our Holy Communion Service (Luke 22:22).

Hallelujah

Everyone fills the fourth glass of wine, and again, psalms are sung: Psalms 115 to 118. The evening ends with the 'Accomplished':

> *Accomplished is the Passover service according to all its laws and statutes. As we have received merit thus to order it, so may we receive merit to fulfil it.*
>
> *O Most Pure, the One who dwells on high, restore the unnumbered congregation of thy people. Speedily lead the offshoots of the plant which you have planted, as a redeemed people, unto Zion with joyous song.*

All say together:
NEXT YEAR IN JERUSALEM!

Printed in the United Kingdom
by Lightning Source UK Ltd.
128854UK00001B/64-291/P

9 780954 970888